Tube Flies

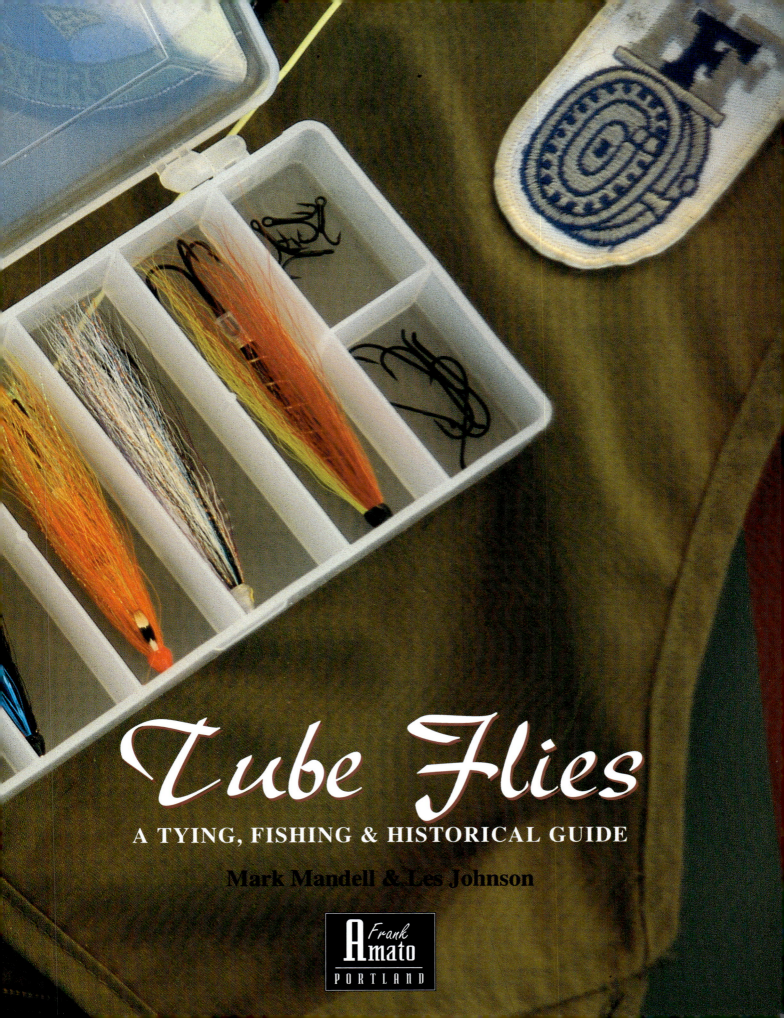

Tube Flies

A TYING, FISHING & HISTORICAL GUIDE

Mark Mandell & Les Johnson

Frank
Amato
PORTLAND

DEDICATION

This book is dedicated to the memory of my dear aunt and uncle, Josephine and Charles Sebolt, who taught me, among many other things, to fish.

Mark Mandell

In memory of my grandfather, Edward J. Knight, an angler of exceptional skill who found merit in every facet of sport fishing. We spent many a day together, fishing for everything from freshwater panfish to salmon in the salt. I'm sure that upon trying tube flies he'd have found them to be "a bit of all right."

Les Johnson

Published in 1995 by Frank Amato Publications, Inc.
P.O. Box 82112, Portland, Oregon 97282
(503) 653-8108

Front and back cover photographs: Jim Schollmeyer
Title page photograph: Les Johnson
Tube fly plate photography: Jim Schollmeyer
Instructional tube fly tying sequence photography: Les Johnson
All other photos credited
Line drawings: Les Johnson

Softbound ISBN: 1-57188-036-4
Softbound UPC: 0-66066-00227-3

Hardbound ISBN: 1-57188-037-2
Hardbound UPC: 0-66066-00228-0

Book Design: Tony Amato

Printed in Hong Kong

3   5   7   9   10   8   6   4   2

TABLE OF CONTENTS

FOREWORD

I suppose the most surprising thing about this book is that it wasn't written sooner. For reasons I don't understand, tube flies have never really caught on in the United States. Europeans have long known the effectiveness of tube flies and used them in much of their fishing. Charles Ritz of Paris gave me some Atlantic salmon flies during the early 1970s, urging me to use them on the Alta River. I did, and they were the most effective patterns on the river that week.

There are a host of reasons for using tube flies. They make it so simple to change patterns to meet conditions. There is no need to carry large boxes of flies mounted on their own hooks. Instead, a small assortment of hooks and liberal supply of tube flies can be carried in an incredibly small box. In the area of salt-water fly fishing, large flies are often called for. Tube flies can easily satisfy the requirement for making very long flies that are easy to cast. By using a lengthy tube and dressing most of it, extended bodies can be easily made that are light, easy to cast, and will tempt larger species. Perhaps the biggest drawback to making popping bugs of considerable size and length is that there are no hooks with shanks long enough. Again, the tube popping bug is the ultimate answer.

I could go on explaining why tube flies will work in nearly every area of fly fishing. But, Mark Mandell and Les Johnson have a mission—to make other fly fishers aware of the value of using tube flies. Read this book and then put into practice many of their suggestions and I promise you that your fishing success will improve.

Lefty Kreh

To the surprise of those who have made, used or studied them, tube flies have never been seen or heard of by many serious fly rod anglers.

Mark Mandell and Les Johnson's book will work for both beginners and masters of the field. This is good writing on a thoroughly researched and practiced subject. Not only does this work detail construction and tying procedures for master or beginner, but it is sure to point up uses for tube flies where they may never have been seen.

Veteran anglers will be surprised at the versatility of the "medium"—and new fly casters will be surprised at the simplicity of some of the approaches. Even those who have long used tube arrangements of one kind or another will be surprised at the extended capabilities of tubes, hair and feathers.

The authors emphasize the practical advantages of the flies—and a reader may suddenly realize that the tube business would cover all or nearly all of his angling, especially if he deals in fairly large flies and fairly large fish. Schools of bluefish or northern pike can be fatal to conventional attractions, and the overhead becomes noticeable when fishing is good. It is comforting to have an ornate creation simply slide up and out of the way instead of being chewed to oblivion.

Catch and release becomes more practical with toothy catches when the hook can be abandoned with no harm to the part that attracted the fish. And some of the flies described are more delicate than most readers would expect.

The stories of people who have introduced tube patterns and construction methods are an added attraction to *Tube Flies* and a surprising share of the angling famous have had a part in their development.

With this book in print it appears there isn't much need for another text on the subject for some time.

Charles F. Waterman

ACKNOWLEDGMENTS

This book is the first we know of that is devoted entirely to tube flies. With few prior writings to use as reference, we counted heavily on the generous outpouring of support from a great many people. Some of the contributors to *Tube Flies* are well known in fly fishing circles while others from various corners of the world are not household names, but are equally skilled and creative tube fly tiers. Whatever *Tube Flies* imparts to the reader in terms of fly tying or interesting personal angling vignettes is due in large measure to these people who took time from their busy schedules to give us a helping hand.

For their exceptional contributions and patience throughout this project, a few individuals must be singled out. Lefty Kreh made himself available from the outset to help us define the scope of the book and provided clues that enabled us to track down the originators of some of the patterns. Bill Hunter contributed not only his Atlantic salmon fly patterns which have been proven around the world, but a selection of excellent photos. Rod Yerger, one of America's premier professional fly tiers, dressed many of the Atlantic salmon flies in this book and helped us track down information whenever we asked, filling in many historical gaps in the text. Our good fortune to be able to include the work of internationally known fly tier Davy Wotton cannot be too strongly stated. Alan Bramley of Partridge of Redditch and Rudi Heger of Traun River Products were solid supporters of the project from the very start, and provided us with fly patterns, and samples of tubes, hooks, and materials. Mark Waslick and Joe Butorac, who dressed their tube fly and popper patterns for the tying instruction sequences, were most gracious, repeating some of the steps many times to ensure that we had recorded them correctly.

We thank you, one and all.

INTRODUCTION

In July 1988, I was part of a group of about a dozen anglers from the Pacific Northwest who spent a week in Loreto, Baja California Sur, Mexico, fly fishing the sargasso patties of the Sea of Cortez for dorado. Before the trip was half over, strikes by hordes of dorado to 40 pounds had reduced our stash of commercially-tied, wooden surface poppers to splinters and bare hooks. Even worse, many of the fish we landed couldn't be released because they'd taken the popper so deeply it was impossible to remove it without doing them a mortal injury.

Upon our return home, a few members of the group began experimenting with a popping bug that would better withstand the punishment of big saltwater fish. Given the crushing power of the dorado's jaws and its dental wherewithall, avoiding the punishment seemed the easiest way around the problem. Like many American fly tiers, our first exposure to flies built on tubes came from the ground-breaking book, *Fly Fishing for Pacific Salmon* (Frank Amato Publications, Inc., 1985), which Les Johnson co-authored with Bruce Ferguson and Pat Trotter. With this idea as an inspiration, in isolation—and ignorance of what tiers elsewhere were doing—we began making poppers on hard plastic tubes that slid up the leader on the strike.

Les Johnson joined the group's trip to Loreto in 1991, where he and I were roommates and fishing partners. In the process of gearing up for the adventure, we met Joe Butorac, a professional fly tier from Arlington, Washington. On a visit to Port Townsend early in 1991, Joe generously shared with us the techniques he had developed in his 25 years of tying saltwater tube poppers.

In 1991 our tube poppers caught lots of fish, and though we had trouble getting off-the-shelf enamel spray paint to stay on the ethafoam heads we were using, the poppers did slide up the line when hit and continued to float after countless maulings.

The big problem this trip was that our conventional Lefty's Deceivers only lasted one or two fish because the hooks were taken so hard and so deep that getting them out required pliers and the operation turned the fly and the curve of the hook into a corkscrewed mess. The solution sat right across the dinner table from us at the Hotel Oasis, in the persons of Swedish anglers and tiers Roland Holmberg and Gunnar Lindback. With their very limited stock of streamer tube flies, Roland and Gunnar got amazing results on both dorado and billfish. Though Les had already had considerable experience with streamer tube flies—in 1984 he began manufacturing and selling them under the Tidemark logo to the salmon sportfishing fleet in the San Francisco Bay area—Roland and Gunnar gave us all our first glimpse of the potential versatility of a full, tube fly system.

After returning to the States, we did some research and verified what we already suspected: For 50 years, with little recognition and no acclaim, fly fishers and tiers all over the world had been exploring tubular possibilities in both fresh and saltwater. Though it crashed dreams of a particular kind of glory (we were not the fly tying Einsteins we thought we were), it made us want to find out more. Who were these original tube tiers? What were their patterns? And what were today's cutting edge tube tiers doing?

The other thing we discovered was that, though tube flies had been mentioned in other works (*Saltwater Fly Patterns*, compiled by Lefty Kreh, Maral, Inc.; *Atlantic Salmon Flies and Fishing* by Joseph Bates, Stackpole Books, 1970), there had never been an entire book devoted to the subject. We resolved to do something about that.

In the winter of 1992, on the Olympic Peninsula's Hoh River, we warmed our boots in front of a smoldering, drizzle-soaked campfire and began to plan this project. We had already come to grips with one of the immediate difficulties: the Einstein Quotient. Because tube fly tying has been so little publicized, because it has been carried out in isolation; because there has never been any book-length work on the subject, let alone an authoritative one; because differences between so-called "patterns" can be slight, determining who "invented" what becomes a vague and extremely touchy matter. We are indebted to Lefty Kreh who graciously reviewed some of the "new patterns" we'd been using and put us on to their real originators. We are also grateful for his suggestion that Atlantic salmon tube flies be covered in this book.

We realized very early on in this project that, for the reasons listed above, it was almost guaranteed that we were going to miss some tiers and flies that should be in this book. While this didn't, and doesn't, sit well with us, the alternative was to not write the book at all; and we know the only way to clarify matters is to expose them to the light of day, to take our lumps and apologize if we have slighted anybody.

A final word: Our goal was never to present a comprehensive work on tube flies—given the explosion in new materials and applications, given the heretofore "closet" nature of tube tiers such a thing is simply not possible. Our goal was to give you a look at tube flies, past and present. And we've included samples of tube flies (that work!) from a few anglers relatively new to tube fly tying. We did this to demonstrate that innovation isn't the private domain of the "experts." Even though we provide tying recipes (some of them lengthy and detailed) for specific flies, understanding the tying techniques and uses of new materials is much more important than how much bucktail or what color of Krystal Flash goes into a particular fly. If you understand the techniques and applications, you can begin to express your own vision. Only if *Tube Flies* encourages you to explore the limits of the format and materials will we consider it a success.

Mark Mandell and Les Johnson
November 30, 1994

1

GOING TUBULAR

As angling consumers with disposable income, we are all deluged with material imperatives, mostly unstated, to the effect that if we don't have the latest doodad of gear, a particular brand of new doodad, we aren't *really* fly fishing. Such calls might appeal to the insecure packrat in us, and they do help keep people employed, but they have little to do with what the sport is about: a river, fog-shrouded and swirling icy cold around your knees; the tropical sun dawning like Armageddon over a slate and vermillion sea; the look on an eight-year-old's face when that first ten-inch trout rises to a fly she or he has tied. This book about tube flies relates to the above treasures, forever freeze-framed in memory, in the same way as neoprene waders, as polarized glasses, as fly floatant. And having admitted the unthinkable, that what we intend to dispense is not absolutely indispensable to the fulfillment and savor of a fly fisher's life, we must still answer the Big Question: Why should you even *consider* tying and fishing tube flies?

We think there are several very good reasons.

A hen steelhead, half submerged, awaits release. Hanging from her jaw is Heger's Shrimp-Leech tube fly. Rudi Heger photo

Tube Flies Simplify Your Tackle

You can carry a large selection of tube flies in a small space. And that space doesn't also have to accommodate razor sharp hooks, which can be carried in a separate hook safe. With tubes, it is possible to carry enough flies for a whole day's fishing in your shirt pocket. You also need fewer hooks, as one hook can be switched from fly to fly.

Tube Flies Allow You to Quickly Adjust to Changing Fishing Conditions

A single tube fly can be adapted to situations that would normally require many different flies tied on different sizes and styles of hook. With tubes, you can switch hook sizes and styles by retying one knot. If, for example, you are river fishing and find yourself hooking smolt after smolt, you can tie a bigger hook on the same fly. If you keep missing solid, on-the-eyeballs hits on your saltwater popper, you can switch to a hook with a shorter shank or wider gap. When you're fishing a deep-sinking fly over a snaggy river bottom, you can reduce your hang-ups by changing to a hook with a smaller gap. Fishing tube poppers for freshwater bass, you can quickly replace a regular hook with one pre-tied with a weedguard.

You can also turn a subsurface tube fly into a surface popper, or vice versa, by simply adding or removing a foam or balsa popper head. Similarly, you can make a subsurface fly into a deep sinker by putting on a heavier hook, or depending on the type of tube fly you tie, by pushing a length of metal tube into the back of the head. Or you can create a dedicated fast sinker by tying the fly on metal tubes of various lengths and diameters. With a tube fly you can also adjust the position of the hookpoint relative to the tail of the fly. This can be important with long baitfish imitations and touchy, short-striking game fish.

Tube Flies Last Much Longer Than Conventional Hook-Tied Flies

Obviously, no fly is indestructible. And a fly's survival usually depends on how deeply it is taken by a fish. But on-average, our estimate is that a tube fly will last at least twice as long as a conventional fly.

The "why" of this is easy to visualize. Tube flies slip up the leader on the strike, away from a hooked fish's teeth. The pair of Holmberg Sea Habits shown in the accompanying photo were retired after they had taken 12 bonito (third fly from top), and 17 skipjack tuna to eight pounds (bottom fly), respectively. While the Mylar piping-sleeved body of the upper Sea Habit tied on a copper tube is chewed to smithereens—since metal tubes are heavier, they tend to stay closer to a fish's mouth than plastic tubes—its wing and jungle cock eyes are still perfect. The bottom fly tied on the plastic tube is in even better shape.

The only downside of a fly that slips up the leader is the possibility that a following fish may strike it and cut the line—in our experience on the west coast of the U.S. this is a very uncommon event. This could be a much more serious drawback on the east coast with bluefish about, although a tube fly can be stopped (see "Rigging" in the Materials chapter) so it doesn't move very far up the line. Because each tube fly lasts longer, you need tie and carry fewer flies. If you know your product is going to survive a couple of dozen fish, using the best materials and spending a half hour on a single fly to get it right makes sense.

Tube Flies Make Catch-and-Release Fishing Much Easier

With a deeply hooked fish, you can save your fly by sliding it up the leader and clipping off the hook; the fish can then be released without bringing it into the boat avoiding risk of further

Tube flies last longer! On top is an unfished painted ethafoam tube popper and beneath it is a similar popper after a full day's dorado fishing. The fourth fly is a prototype balsa tube slider that was still floating after innumerable strikes by dorado, cabrilla, and big needlefish. Below that is a tube Calamarko that took more than 20 coho and pink salmon in the Strait of Juan de Fuca. The third and fifth flies, Holmberg Sea Habits, took a total of 29 bonito and skipjack.

injury. Tie on a new hook and you're quickly back in business with a fly you have confidence in (we all know that some flies fish better than others). Since you aren't tying directly on the hook and hook replacement is so simple, it's practical to use a hook that will quickly corrode in salt or freshwater.

There is also the question of injury to the fly fisher practicing catch-and-release. When fishing for sharks, wahoo, or other aggressive, well-armed saltwater species it is a definite advantage to be able to slide the fly up the leader and cut the line a safe distance from the hook eye and the fish's mouth, saving the bug, the fish, and avoiding potential damage to the fingers.

Tube Flies Replicate Baitfish in a Way That Hook-Tied Flies Can't

Tube flies offer a more realistic body silhouette, sleek and translucent like a real baitfish in the water. Since most tubes are much larger in diameter than any hook shank, the wing and body material flows back from a broad head and shoulder to a natural point at the tail, giving the *appearance* of more bulk without

Note the well-chewed ethafoam popper has slipped up the leader as Mandell prepares to tail a dorado. Les Johnson photo

The dorado is tailed, to be quickly released alive. Les Johnson photo

The herring on the tackle box was spit out by a Neah Bay coho caught on a Capitán Skippy's Little Coho. Note the matching size of the fly and the natural bait. The Little Coho's extended gill plates of silver Mylar piping give its head and shoulder a realistic contour and flash. Les Johnson photo

added weight. The size of the fly is not limited by the length or diameter of the hook shank; insofar as tying is concerned, the hook shank is irrelevant. This means a five-inch fly can take a very short hook that doesn't interfere with the natural movement of its wing and body materials.

We've made five claims in favor of the wider use of tube flies. Some of the plusses—modular capability, increased fly longevity, and easier catch-and-release—seem obvious, even at first glance. We trust the other advantages we've mentioned in this chapter will become equally apparent as you read on.

To start with, we're going take you through the materials and tools necessary for tube fly tying. Next, we'll present step-by-step instruction in the tying of the four basic types of tube fly covered in this book: the Atlantic salmon fly, the streamer, the slider, and the popper. This is followed by three chapters of pattern recipes that cover tube adaptations of traditional hook-tied flies and original tube flies. Many of the tying instructions include notes from the originators or adaptors on the inspiration behind the pattern, tying techniques, and fishing the fly.

2

MATERIALS, TOOLS, RIGGING

This Queen Charlotte Islands' chinook salmon hit a Calamarko pattern. Trey Combs photo

We have to start this chapter with a disclaimer: there's no way to give you a complete list of all the types and colors of material useful for making tube flies. New varieties of established products are coming out weekly, as are applications of previously unheard-of materials. What follows is an overview of the basic requirements for tube fly tying and the materials the tiers featured in this book are using. The addresses of the manufacturers who are listed in this chapter appear in the Appendix. If you're already a fly tier, you probably have much of the wing and body material on hand—a trip to the nearest hardware, hobby, or variety store can put you in business.

TUBING

Tube flies are usually built on short lengths of plastic or metal tubing. The clear plastic tubing discussed in this book falls into two categories: hard and soft. Often, but not always, a tube fly will be built on a joined piece of each. The larger, more flexible,

From top center: ball point pen, ball point pen fillers cut in half, 1/8" hard plastic pressure gauge tubing, 1/8" plastic tubing connected to soft vinyl tubing. Bottom left: Q-Tip stem with 1/8" hard plastic hook holder, Q-Tip, cut Q-Tip stem, hobby shop brass tube lined with Q-Tip. Bottom right: 1/4" colored soft vinyl tubing, three sizes of sleeved copper and aluminum tubes.

soft tubing is pushed over the end of the hard tubing to act as a hook holder. In Atlantic salmon flies, the fly is generally tied only on the hard tubing; other types of tube flies are tied on both the joined hard and soft tubing, and the hook holder is an integral part of the fly body or head. In either case, when a fish strikes, it breaks the grip of the hook holder on the hook eye and the tube fly slips up the leader.

Hard Tubes

The standard clear hard plastic tubing for tube flies is 1/8" O.D. Under the trade name "Slipstream," the British firm of W. T. Humphries and Sons, Ltd. manufactures hard plastic tubes in a variety of lengths specifically for tube fly tying. Slipstream plastic tubes are larger in I.D. at one end; this serves as an internal hook holder for small-eyed hooks. Hard plastic pressure gauge (or carburetor) tubing in 1/8" O.D. is available in auto parts and hardware stores in the U.S. Pressure gauge tubing comes in coils and has a natural curve or set, which in lengths of more than half an inch has to be compensated for before tying begins—otherwise, the finished fly will not track straight on the retrieve. When using this type of tubing, find the natural curve and adjust the tube on your vise so the curve is either pointing straight up or straight down, not off to one side. Joe Butorac favors 1/8" clear chemical lab tubing, which comes in perfectly straight lengths and is much stiffer and more brittle than other types of tubing. This tubing is packaged in the popper kits Joe sells through his Trophy Tackle, Inc. and is also available through medical supply houses.

For the smaller, more delicate flies, an even narrower O.D. hard plastic tubing is preferable. Many tiers cut up the straight plastic tubes in ball point pen refills, and after washing out the ink, build flies on them. Hobby stores sell straight 12" lengths of opaque white plastic tubing in various diameters. You can also use the hollow stems of plastic-handled Q-Tip type swabs.

Soft Tubes

Clear soft tubing is made of vinyl and available in cut-to-suit lengths from large spools in hardware stores in the U.S. Vinyl tubing used by tube tiers is usually 3/16" O.D./1/8" I.D., but smaller flies can require 1/8" O.D. Because this material is sold from large spools, it, too, has a set or curve which must be adjusted for before tying begins. This means matching up the curve of the soft tubing with the curve, if any, of the hard tubing before you join them, and then adjusting the connected tubing on your vise so the curve is up or down. It helps to mark the top of the tube in some way to keep your up/down reference point. Either a few fibers of contrasting bucktail or FisHair along the spine, or a pencil or pen mark on the front tip of the tube will work fine. Short pieces of colored vinyl tubing (fluorescent red, yellow, green), are also available at bait and tackle stores that sell lure building supplies.

Connected to 1/8" I.D. soft vinyl hook holders, from top: 1/8" O.D. hard plastic tubing, 1/8" lined copper tubing, and lined hobby shop brass tubing.

Keyholing

It is possible to keyhole the end of hard plastic (except chemical lab tubing) or soft vinyl tubing to fit a particular hook eye. This makes it easier to connect the tube and hook eye, especially with large saltwater hooks, and you are less likely to tear the plastic tubing with repeated hook insertions and removals. Before you start tying, heat the end of the plastic tube in boiling water for a few seconds, then, adjusting for the curve of the tubing, push the softened end over the hook eye.

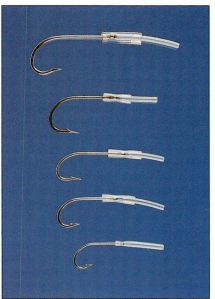

Keyholed tubes, from top: Eagle Claw DO67 5/0 in 1/4" O.D. (1/8" I.D.) soft vinyl tubing; Mustad 34007 4/0 in 3/16" O.D. soft vinyl; Eagle Claw DO67 3/0 in 3/16" O.D. soft vinyl; Eagle Claw DO67 2/0 in 3/16" O.D. soft vinyl; Eagle Claw DO67 Size 1 in 1/8" O.D. hard plastic tubing.

The thin-walled plastic or vinyl will reform around the eye. Quench the tubing in cold water. Once you've swaged the tube in this way, proceed with the pattern, making sure the keyhole is perpendicular to the top of the fly.

Metal Tubes

Metal tubes in 1/8" O.D. are also commonly used for tube fly tying. You can adjust the sink of a fly to water conditions by changing the length of the tube and the type of metal it is made of. Slow-sinking or neutrally-buoyant, plastic-lined aluminum tubes are produced specifically for fly tying in different lengths by Slipstream and by Traun River Products. Slipstream also makes lined copper and brass tubes that are fast sinkers. For whatever metal is involved, a soft plastic liner is critical because it keeps the edge of the metal tube from rubbing against and fraying the leader. Hobby stores sell all three kinds of metal tubing in 12" lengths and various diameters. You can line metal tubes with 1.75 or 1.5mm O.D. clear teflon tubing which is available from medical or scientific instrument supply companies. Cut the teflon liner a bit longer than the tube, insert it, then carefully soften the ends in a candle flame and flatten them to lock the liner in place.

In some countries, flies are tied on brass and copper tubes up to four inches long. These quick-sinking metal tubes will reach fish holding in the deepest and heaviest pools of large rivers.

Because of the additional weight, brass and copper tube flies can be perilous both to rod and caster, and a two-handed rod is usually required to handle them.

Wing Materials

The winging materials employed in tube flies are the same as for conventional flies. Natural fibers include saddle hackles, bucktail, polar bear, African goat, Arctic fox, and monkey. Because the tiers in this book are from around the world, some of the natural material called for in their fly patterns may not be legal to import or possess in your country—polar bear and monkey fur specifically come to mind. If this is the case, just substitute an appropriate synthetic.

A selection of synthetic winging material from Traun River Products (Germany) and Umpqua Feather Merchants (Glide, Oregon).

As with conventional flies, tube tiers use synthetic winging materials to substitute for illegal or expensive items. The standard hair substitutes are FisHair, Ultra Hair, Super Hair, and Ocean Hair. Each of these products has slightly different properties: more or less translucence, flexibility, bulk, sparkle, etc. In the pattern chapters of this book, the individual tier's notes discuss the application of some of these materials to specific water conditions and angling situations. Also employed as wing material on tube flies, but more often added for color and flash, are the Mylar fibers sold under various names: Flashabou, Flashabou Accent, Spectraflash, Krystal Flash, and others. The packagers of this material have it dyed to their own specifications, so there are a wide variety of tints, hues, and combinations of pearlescent and metallic colors available.

Piping

Most fly tiers are familiar with the smaller diameters of pearl, silver, and gold Mylar piping used to make Muddler, Zonker, and other streamer bodies on hook-tied flies. Braided Mylar piping is often used in tube flies, either on the body, the head, or both. The diameter of Mylar piping doesn't expand very far; but when it's tied down at one end of a tube and stretched, it

A selection of mylar piping.

compresses nicely, so medium size piping will work for small and medium tubes, likewise large piping will work for medium tubes. In the fly recipe chapters we have noted the size of piping the tier uses, but you can almost always go one size larger without concern.

Sleeving the heads of tube poppers, sliders, and big streamers calls for the largest available Mylar piping. Minnow Body Large is bigger than pearl Mylar extra large, and the Mylar fibers in Minnow Body are finer and more active in the water. Minnow Body comes in pearl and a variety of braided pearl and metallic colors.

When the dorsal of a popper or a slider head is painted black, then sleeved with braided Mylar and epoxied, the result is a prismatic effect. Depending on your angle of view, the head is iridescent gold/green, or green striped with bright blue. Other combinations of undercolors and piping give different effects (see "Balsa Tube Poppers" in Popper chapter). Various dyed colors of pearlescent Mylar piping are also available, as is a phosphorescent or glow-in-the-dark piping, trade-named Everglow, which comes in white, red, orange, yellow, and green.

No size standard exists between these different types of piping. For example, Everglow extra large isn't as big as Minnow Body Large, and because the fibers of Everglow are wider and stiffer, they expand even less. It always pays to check the maximum I.D. of the sleeve you intend to use before you start tying. There is a way to get around having too small a piping for the job at hand, and this is addressed later in the book.

Less well known than the all-Mylar braids are the new plastic and combination plastic/Mylar braids like Flexo PET and Flexo Mirror Braid. PET is used to sheath and protect marine electrical cables and Mirror Braid is used by custom car buffs to dress up the tubing and cables in their engine compartments. PET comes in clear and a variety of single and mixed colors; Mirror Braid is clear/silver. On popper and streamer heads they can be used to create a scale effect. This material has a couple of advantages over the standard Mylar piping used for fly tying. PET is light, yet incredibly tough—to trim it use sidecutters, it kills fly tying scissors! Unlike Mylar braid, it

A selection of Flexo material and four fly heads sleeved with it.

expands to fit large diameters (the 1/2" size stretches to 7/8")
and as it expands, its mesh opens up, allowing the underbody
material to show through. To get this show-through effect it's
better use smaller sizes of Flexo expanded to the maximum. The
1/2" Mirror Braid is just right for a 7/8" diameter, billfish popper
head. Flexo is manufactured by Techflex, Inc. and is available
through marine electronics and supply stores in the U.S.

*Poppers and sliders painted, then sleeved with various types of mylar
piping. Les Johnson photo*

Thread

The only thread currently involved in tube fly tying that is
new or different is clear monofilament sewing thread. This
product takes some getting used to because of the memory of
the mono and its tendency to slip off the tube if you let the
bobbin tension go slack. The transparency of the mono once
it's been epoxied allows you to make some very interesting fly
heads. It also makes it possible to use a sheet or flattened piece
of Mylar piping to cover a fly head when you don't have the
proper size of piping for the fly you're tying. This technique is
first described in the streamer pattern chapter, under the tube
version of Errol Champion's Salmon Treat.

*Lifelike, two-tone fly heads can be created using clear monofilament
sewing thread.*

*Les Johnson and a 14-pound Queen Charlotte chum salmon taken on
the Holmberg Sea Habit in 1993. Trey Combs photo*

Popper and Slider Heads

Popper and slider heads for tube flies can be made of a number of different materials: ethafoam, Live Body foam, striped foam, plastic, and balsa.

White ethafoam makes extremely light, high-floating heads, and is used in Joe Butorac's tube fly standard, the Pop-Eyed Popper, described in the "Basic Tying Steps" chapter. Tube popper kits containing these heads are available through Joe Butorac's Trophy Tackle.

Live Body is a much denser foam material that floats lower in the water than ethafoam. Because of its extra weight, Live Body makes a popper that is a bit heavier and a little more difficult to cast. On the other hand, it better resists fish teeth and is easier to shape if you are making a slider head. Detailed instructions for shaping and working with this material are found under Mark Waslick's Bait Slider in the "Basic Tying Steps" chapter. Live Body can be colored with a permanent marker. It is available in a variety of colors and diameters from the manufacturer, Dale Clemens Custom Tackle.

The newest heads on the market are the tiger-striped, blue/white, black/white, red/black, green/black, and purple/black foam poppers and sliders from Peter Hylander of Seattle Saltwater, who also sells popper tube fly kits. Trophy Tackle produces molded plastic slider heads in different sizes. These are used in Joe Butorac's commercially-tied Flasher Fly (intended for coho salmon) and Trophy Slider (for all saltwater game fish).

You can also build your own tube slider and popper heads from sheet balsa. Detailed instructions for constructing, shaping, and finishing balsa heads are found in the popper chapter.

A selection of foam popper heads. On the left are four solid color Live Body heads from Dale Clemens Custom Tackle. The other painted and variegated foam heads are manufactured by Seattle Saltwater.

Body, Ribbing, and Eyes

In general, this is the same floss, wool, fur dubbing, spun deer hair, and chenille used in conventional flies. Some of the products listed in the fly patterns may not be familiar to you, however.

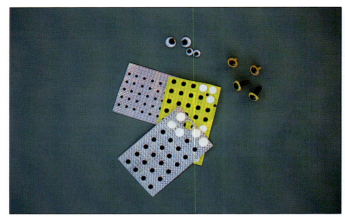

Stick-on Witchcraft Mylar eyes, plastic doll's eyes with flat backs, and plastic doll's eyes with back posts are all popular with tube fly tiers.

Spectrachenille, from Rudi Heger's Traun River Products, is a chenille made of short strips of pearl Mylar and dyed various colors. Flexibody is a sheet plastic material used for orange and red shell-backs in Davy Wotton's shrimp and prawn Atlantic salmon patterns. It comes in 20 colors. Davy's Flashback is a clear, pearlescent, sheet plastic material that can be colored with a waterproof marker—this is used on translucent versions of Wotton's SLF prawn flies. SLF is a seal fur substitute, also developed and produced by Davy Wotton and distributed by Partridge of Redditch; it is sold as dubbing and in hanks (short, straight lengths).

The flies in this book employ two types of plastic doll's eyes: those with movable pupils and no backposts, and those with fixed pupils and backposts. Many tiers like various sizes of Witchcraft eyes which are printed on sheets of adhesive-backed Mylar. Glass or plastic beads strung on monofilament are also used.

Vises

At present there are three commercially-produced tube vises on the market. The Jack Perry vise has been manufactured since 1988 and is the most widely used. It is designed to fit any standard clamp or pedestal base. Two new tube fly vises have recently entered the picture. The Bill Hunter-designed Tube Fly Tying Tool, (see Hunter's patterns in the Atlantic Salmon Tube Flies chapter) manufactured by Kennebec River Fly and Tackle Co., fits between the jaws of a standard tying vise. It comes with three steel pins sized to fit various diameters of tubing. A threaded nut supplies downward pressure to the pin, which holds the end of the tube clamped against the vise's frame. Seattle Saltwater makes tube adaptors machined to fit the Renzetti Traveler and Regal vises.

Any of these vises will give you good service, but tube fly tying doesn't require you invest in one. There are many ways to make a tube fly adapter to fit your standard vise. Joe Butorac takes a 6" embroidery needle, sold in bubble packs of two, and slightly roughens the pointed half of the needle with a file. Then he simply fits the eye end into his standard vise. If the tube fly you're tying has an attached hook holder, you can follow Mark

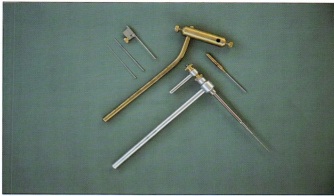

Vises for tube flies. From left: the HMH Tube Fly Tying Tool with three mandrels from Kennebec River Fly and Tackle Co., the Perry Vise with removable mandrel, the Seattle Saltwater tube adapter (shown in a Renzetti Traveler vise).

Waslick's example and put a hook in your standard vise, shove the hook holder end of the tube over the eye, and start tying. Other make-do adapters that contributors have suggested are cotter pins and the steel handle shanks of metal files.

Hooks for Tube Flies

In the research for this book, we have found only two designated "tube fly hooks," both manufactured by Partridge of Redditch. The Peter Masting (or P.M.) hook is a japanned treble with a straight extension welded onto it that fits into the tube body to maintain proper alignment. Masting is a renowned rod on the River Tay in Scotland. The Alan Bramley (or A.B.) hook is a treble designed for sea trout. Although there are currently only two dedicated tube fly hooks, many different styles of standard hooks work just fine on tube flies. In fact, our advice is to try whatever hooks you already have on hand. And before you buy new hooks for tube flies, check the fit of the hook eye into the tubing you intend to use.

Though almost any hook of proper size for the fly will work, those with ring or straight eyes are easier to deal with if you are using a hook holder. You can use an up or down eye hook as well, but you should snell the leader behind the eye, and snug the hook eye up tight against it—that way, the leader is pulling against the hook shank, not the eye. This properly aligns the hook point so it rides straight behind the fly, instead of either cocked up or down. If you are not using a hook holder, you can cut the rear end of the hard tubing at a 45° angle as Joe Butorac does, to accommodate the up-eyed, short shank, bait hooks he recommends for some of his flies. Bruce Ferguson of Gig Harbor, Washington, a long-time tube fly fisher, also likes an offset, plated, short shank, salmon/steelhead bait hook (no slices on the shank) on his saltwater tubes. He thinks the offset hook gives the fly better action. Mark Bale of Bellevue, Washington, employs a snelled, offset, up eye bait hook on his Bale Tube Fly (see Streamer chapter).

That said, we are going to mention some specific brands and model numbers of hooks that have worked well for us and for

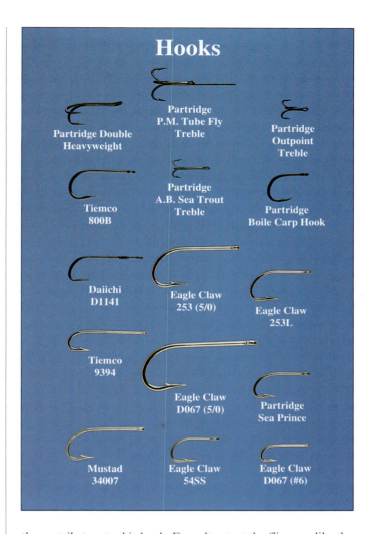

Hooks

Partridge Double Heavyweight

Partridge P.M. Tube Fly Treble

Partridge Outpoint Treble

Tiemco 800B

Partridge A.B. Sea Trout Treble

Partridge Boile Carp Hook

Daiichi D1141

Eagle Claw 253 (5/0)

Eagle Claw 253L

Tiemco 9394

Eagle Claw D067 (5/0)

Partridge Sea Prince

Mustad 34007

Eagle Claw 54SS

Eagle Claw D067 (#6)

the contributors to this book. For saltwater tube flies, we like the Eagle Claw 253 because it has a small ring eye, is light in large sizes (4/0 or 5/0), yet has proven strong enough even in small sizes (1 or 1/0) for most saltwater fish. It is a dependable and inexpensive laser-sharpened hook. (Remember, with a tube fly the hook is expendable! On a deeply-hooked fish, just slide the tube fly up the leader and cut off the hook.) The larger ring eyes of the Eagle Claw extra strong Billy Pate Model D067 sizes 1/0 through 3/0 keyhole nicely into thin-walled, 3/16" O.D. vinyl hook holders; the 3/0 to 5/0 size (for tarpon and billfish) fit in keyholed 1/4" O.D./1/8" I.D. tubing. Other good single hooks for saltwater tubes include the Mustad 3407/34007, the Partridge Sea Prince, the Eagle Claw 54SS, and the Tiemco 800S.

Freshwater single hooks we have tried include the Kevin Maddock's Boile Carp Hook (short shank, extra strong, wide gap, japanned finish) by Partridge, the Tiemco 800B, and the Daiichi 1141 (return loop, straight eye, japanned finish). To use a loop eye hook like the Daiichi on a tube fly, whip finish the open eye of the loop and cement the wraps. For single salmon hooks, the Partridge M and N, Daiichi 1141, and Mustad 36980 are all excellent. Many tube fly fishers prefer the Outpoint Trebles from Partridge for Atlantic salmon fishing.

Rigging

The rigging of tube flies can be accomplished in several different ways. On a tube fly built without a hook holder, like Holmberg's Sea Habit, the fly is strung up the leader and the hook is tied on and left to swing freely behind the tube. Saltwater tube flies without hook holders sometimes have a glass or plastic bead strung between the end of the tube and the hook eye, to act as a bearing. On tube flies with hook holders, after the fly is run up the line, the single, double, or treble hook

Rubber bobber stops can be placed as shown to control a tube fly's movement on the leader.

Rigging for tube flies. From left: the Pop-Eyed Popper has a double (5/0) hook rig for billfish. The Sea Habit Atlantic salmon fly is rigged with a free-swinging rear single hook (Note: it has no hook holder). The pair of tube streamers are both are built on joined pieces of hard and soft tubing. The streamer on the left has a length of clear hard plastic tubing shoved in its hook holder to adjust the position of the hook point. At the right is an Atlantic salmon fly with a hook holder swaged to take a treble hook.

is tied to the leader, then the eye is snugged up into the holder. This also works with a double-hook, billfish rig.

To keep the tube from sliding too far up the leader, or slipping at all, Joe Butorac uses a bobber float stop, sold on small spools in bait and tackle stores to fit a range of line diameters. This tiny piece of perforated rubber is slid onto the leader ahead of the fly. After the hook is tied on, the rubber stop is moved down against the nose of the fly, restricting its forward movement on the leader. When there is no hook holder on the fly, a bobber float stop can also be used to adjust the distance between the rear of the tube and the hook eye, which can be important with short-striking fish. A similar adjustment can be made on tubes with hook holders by inserting a piece of 1/8" tubing of the desired length into the soft tubing.

3

BASIC TYING STEPS

In two years of research for this project, we ran across conventional fly tiers who, at one time or another, had tried on their own to figure out how to tie flies on tubes, but couldn't seem to get the hang of it and soon gave up. Their experiences told us we couldn't get by with the materials-list-and-fly-plate-photo approach of a standard tying book.

Our goal is to get you to start thinking in tubular terms; before you can do that, you have to be able to tie accurate replicas of the tube flies we've featured. To help ensure everyone's success, we've done our best to make all written instructions complete and precise, and the fly photos as detailed as possible.

The Basic Tying Steps section begins with a standard Atlantic salmon tube fly, then proceeds to more difficult patterns, both in the balance and blending of materials, and in the manual dexterity required to assemble them. These photo sequences will give you the fundamentals for tying all Atlantic salmon, streamer, slider, and popper tube flies covered in this book. They are the same steps you'll use to create your own tube fly pattern.

The Atlantic salmon step-by-step sequence was tied by the authors; the other three sequences were prepared with the help of two fine U.S. fly tiers and tube innovators, Mark Waslick and Joe Butorac.

THE ATLANTIC SALMON TUBE FLY

Hairy Mary

A standard British Atlantic salmon pattern.
Tubing: 2" of 1/8" hard plastic tubing or Slipstream 2" plastic tube, or a 2" aluminum or copper tube. The hook holder is a 1/2" piece of 1/8" O.D. vinyl tubing.
Thread: Black.

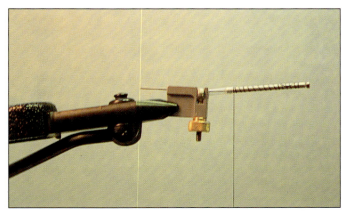

Step 1: Put the joined tube and hook holder on your vise and attach the tying thread.

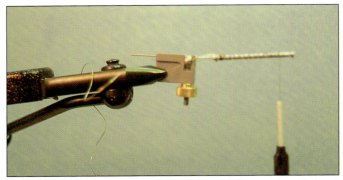

Step 2: On the soft tubing, tie in a piece of fine gold oval tinsel for the tag and rib. Leave enough space for five or six turns of tag between the tie-in point and the front edge of the soft tubing.

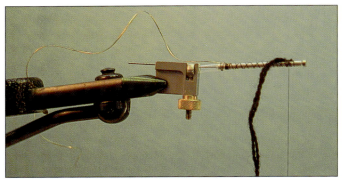

Step 3: Wrap the thread forward to 1/4" from the front end and tie in a piece of black floss or wool.

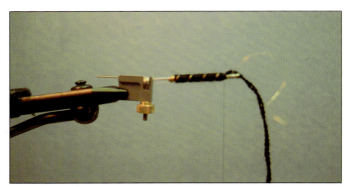

Step 4: Wind the black floss down the tube to the edge of the soft tubing, then back to the head of the fly. Tie it off at the head. Wrap a tag of six turns of oval tinsel, then continue to rib forward over the body with five or six turns of oval tinsel to the head, tie it down, and trim the excess tinsel and floss.

Step 5: Tie a small bunch of natural brown bucktail or fox squirrel on the top of the tube, making the tips of the wing extend slightly past the end of a hook inserted in the hook holder.

Step 6: Rotate the tube in the vise 180° so the first wing becomes the belly of the fly. Tie a matching amount of natural brown bucktail on the top of the tube, and make it the same length as the first. Both sides of the body should be visible. Trim the excess bucktail.

Step 7: Tie in a guinea fowl feather dyed bright blue as a front hackle, wet fly style. Make a couple of turns, tie it down, and trim the excess. Complete the fly by making a small, neat head with black thread, whip finish, and lacquer the wraps.

THE STREAMER TUBE FLY

Mark Waslick (Middlebury, Vermont)

After obtaining his Bachelor of Science degree in Wildlife and Fisheries Science from the University of Vermont, Mark Waslick had some free time before starting graduate school. In the eight-month interval, he often spent ten hours a day at the vise, teaching himself to tie classic salmon flies. His exquisite salmon flies (dressed on hooks) have appeared in several fly tying books, notably Joseph Bates' *Art of the Salmon Fly* (David R. Godine) and in the Stewart and Allen series, *Flies for Atlantic Salmon*, *Flies for Steelhead*, and *Flies for Trout* (Northland Press, Inc.). He began working on the Sea Bait tube fly in 1991, inspired by Bob Popovic's Surf Candy and Lani Waller's use of Mylar piping as a sleeve for commercially manufactured popper heads. On the east coasts of the U.S. and Canada, Waslick's Sea Bait streamers, sliders, and poppers in various sizes have caught Arctic char, lake trout, speckled trout, striped bass, bluefish, mackerel, blackfin tuna, dorado, and shark. These flies have also done well in Mexico on tuna, roosterfish, dorado, and cabrilla.

Waslick's Sea Bait

Tubing: 1 1/4" of 1/8" hard plastic tubing and 1/2" of 3/16" vinyl tubing.
Thread: Monocord and 8/0 thread in white.

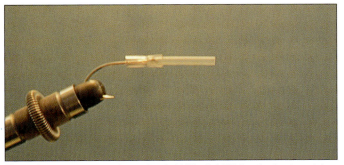

Step 1: Insert approximately 1 1/4" of 1/8" hard plastic tubing into 1/2" of 3/16" vinyl tubing. A drop of Zap-A-Gap will make the bond secure. White monocord is started over this junction of hard and flexible tubes.

Step 2: On the top of the soft tubing, about 3/16" back from its front edge, secure polar bear FisHair (70 Denier Premium) in several very small bunches, one on top of the other. Taper the FisHair to a point by pulling on the center of each bunch before you tie it in. The first two bunches should be the shortest, about 2/3 the overall length of the wing. The third bunch is 1/3 longer than the first two. Tying in this way creates a tapered wing that gives the appearance of bulk, yet is translucent.

Step 3: Rotate the tube 180° in the vise, so the polar bear FisHair becomes the fly's belly. Add eight to ten strands of pearl Krystal Flash to each side, staggering the lengths as with the FisHair.

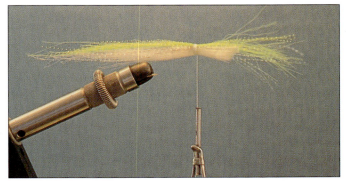

Step 4: On top of the tube, tie in about 1/3 as much chartreuse FisHair as the polar bear, staggering the lengths as you did before. Add 12 or so strands of pearl Krystal Flash over the chartreuse FisHair.

Step 5: Add about half as much polar bear FisHair as the chartreuse to the top of the fly, staggered as before. This layer of polar bear should not entirely obscure the chartreuse.

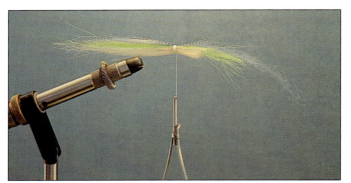

Step 6: Add six strands of pearl Krystal Flash to the top, staggered.

Step 7: On top of that, add an amount of royal blue FisHair, tapered, equal to the last bunch of polar bear FisHair.

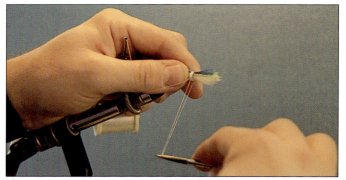

Step 8: Whip finish and apply Zap-A-Gap to the windings.

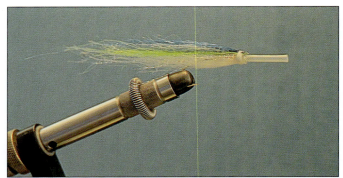

Step 9: When it's dry, trim the ends of the FisHair and Krystal Flash even with the soft tube.

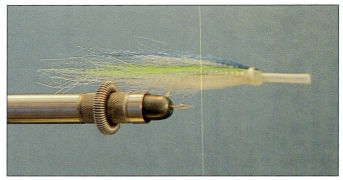

Step 10: Apply 5-minute epoxy from just behind the thread windings to forward of the vinyl tube/hard plastic tube joint. Rotate the fly as the epoxy dries so it takes on the tapered head as in photo (it helps to have a rotary vise.) Just as the epoxy begins to set, it can be molded slightly, if necessary, with your fingers or some other tool. Use vegetable oil, soapy water or alcohol to keep the epoxy from sticking to your hands or tool.

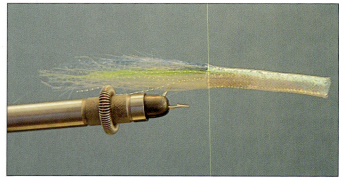

Step 11: When the epoxy dries enough so that it is no longer tacky or sticky to the touch, slip two or three inches of large diameter regular pearl Mylar piping over the tapered head. Make sure the Mylar piping extends far enough back so that epoxy can be applied without getting it on the FisHair wing—slide it an inch or so beyond the tapered head.

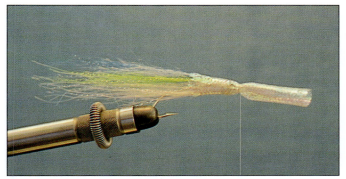

Step 12: With white 8/0 thread, take 1 1/2 turns of very loose wraps around the Mylar before tightening down. Ideally, you want the Mylar to tighten around the stiff tube without folding over onto itself. The nature of the braided Mylar will allow it to reduce its diameter enough to tighten around the stiff tube without folding. It sometimes helps to grasp the Mylar at each end and pull straight out with the right hand slightly, then pull down on the bobbin to secure the Mylar. Lock down the Mylar piping to the hard plastic tube with four or five turns of thread and whip finish. After whip finishing, cut off thread and apply a drop of Zap-A-Gap to the wraps and allow to dry. Draw in the gill lines with red paint or a marking pen.

Step 13: With a sharp single-edge razor blade cut off excess tube and Mylar to the right of the 8/0 thread. Do not use scissors for this—they crush the tube before cutting it and the thread might slip off. A much cleaner cut is made with a razor blade. Use a disposable brush to apply 5-minute epoxy over the head (you get thinner coverage and a lighter fly that way), from the 8/0 thread to a point approximately 1/4" behind the tie-in point of the FisHair. This secures the 8/0 thread, the Mylar and the butts of the FisHair to each other, making the head one unit. Again set your vise for rotary or in-line tying so you can apply the epoxy evenly. With the right hand rotate the vise jaws and fly, and with the left hold a disposable craft brush to apply the epoxy.

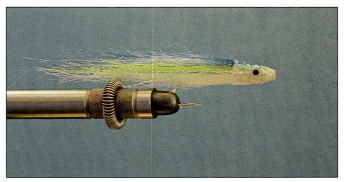

Step 14: When this first coat of epoxy is dry, carefully trim the Mylar behind the head even with the epoxy. Then stick on 1/4" silver Witchcraft eyes and apply a second coat of epoxy. This time allow the epoxy to flow slightly over the edge on the trimmed Mylar and onto the FisHair. This does two things: it makes it look neater and binds the FisHair to the Mylar head, making a very strong head and fly.

Waslick Note: "A shortcut is to apply just one coat of epoxy after you cut the tube with the razor in **Step 13**. Just stick on the eyes and apply epoxy from the 8/0 thread rearward to behind the eyes and let it dry. Trim the Mylar strands. That's it. This still fishes fine, although it's not quite as durable and doesn't look as good. I fish this fly, tied in different sizes, on everything from brookies to stripers. In stillwater I use the FisHair version and in heavy currents I use the Ultrahair version which doesn't tangle as easily."

THE TUBE SLIDER

Waslick's Sea Slider

Tubing: 1/8" hard plastic tubing length is equal to the length of the slider head plus 1/2" to 3/4"; the excess is trimmed after the Mylar piping is attached. Hook holder is 3/8" of 3/16" vinyl tubing.

Thread: Monocord and 8/0 in white.

Step 1: With a variable speed drill and a sanding drum attachment (or by hand on sandpaper), shape the bullet noses at both ends of a piece of white 1/2" or 5/8" diameter Live Body.

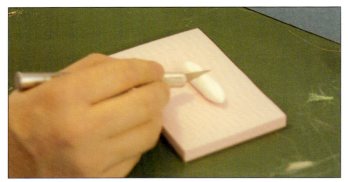

Step 2: Cut the piece of Live Body in half, producing two slider heads.

Step 3: Using the variable speed drill (or by hand), bore out the center of one of the heads with a drill bit matched to the hard tube size (1/8"), then use a 1/4" drill bit (or Dremel bit as shown) to get a bigger bore at rear end so the 3/16" vinyl tubing and thread wraps can slip inside. Put together the lengths of soft and hard tubing (as in Step 1 for the Sea Bait streamer), and wrap down the join area with thread.

Step 4: Apply three white saddle hackles to each side of the tube, leaving the marabou on for a collar. Angle the saddles to form a tent or cove, as shown.

Step 5: On each side apply three chartreuse saddles with marabou in the same manner, on top of the white.

Step 6: Apply six to eight strands of light green Krystal Flash.

Step 7: Build a small tapered head with thread, whip finish, and Zap-A-Gap the wraps.

Step 8: Use paint or permanent marker to color the dorsal surface of the head chartreuse. When it's dry, glue the head onto the tube with Zap-A-Gap.

Step 9: Fray the end of Minnow Body Large Pearl piping, as shown, then slip it over the head so the tips extend past the hook.

Step 10: With a turn or two of thread, tighten down Minnow Body at the join of the slider nose and hard tubing, keeping the rear end of the Minnow Body taut with your fingertips while stretching the front end to narrow the sleeve for a neat fit at the nose.

Step 11: Whip finish, then Zap-A-Gap the wraps. Trim the excess tubing and Minnow Body to the edge of the wraps. Apply silver 5/16" Witchcraft eyes and brush on 5-minute epoxy.

The finished Sea Slider.

THE TUBE POPPER

Joe Butorac (Arlington, Washington)

Joe Butorac first got interested in tube flies in 1959 when his father returned to the San Francisco Bay area from a trip to Seattle with several Puget Sound fishing guide books and some tube trolling flies for coho salmon. After digesting the new information, Joe started applying it to the salmon closer to home. He began tying his own tube flies and fishing them in the ocean out of Pedro Point, 15 miles south of the Golden Gate Bridge, and off the Marin County coast.

Six years later, Joe was living above Mussel Rock, on the coast near Pacifica, California. A few minutes from Joe's front door, gear fishermen were using large surface popping plugs to draw strikes from 20-pound class stripers in the surf line. Joe was eager to hook some of these fish on a fly rod, but after building cork and balsa fly rod poppers on hooks, he had a problem: even with the one-handed 11-weight J. Kennedy Fisher glass rod he was fishing, Joe couldn't easily cast a big enough cork or balsa popper to interest the fish. The combined weight of the popper and a large, long-shanked hook made it very difficult to lift the fly out of the water on the backcast and to then keep it under control in the air.

At the time, Joe was working in the construction industry and was familiar with the 7/8", 5/8", 1/2", and 3/8" diameter cylindrical ethafoam used as spacers for slabs of concrete. The ethafoam was white, incredibly light, and virtually unsinkable. Joe combined this new material with what he had already learned about tube flies: a fly tied on a tube can carry a shorter, lighter hook than a conventional fly. In this way, he solved the casting problems related to popper and hook weight. When Joe began tying poppers with ethafoam, he found it was also very easy to work with, and his combination of a painted ethafoam popper head, saddle hackles, and a short-shanked 5/0 live bait hook was an immediate hit with the surf line stripers.

Joe also liked the extremely high float given by an ethafoam head. When armed with a hook, one of his poppers floats with its nose angled up out of the water at about 45°. Not only does the fly make a prodigous *pop!* when the line is jerked, but if you've ever seen a mortally wounded baitfish on the surface, you know this is often how they skate along, noses in the air, almost like they're trying to climb out of the water.

Joe shared his poppers with his fishing partners, who used them with good success in Baja in the 1970s. In 1982 Joe began to sell Pop-Eyed Poppers commercially through Bill Marts at the Kaufmann's Streamborn store in Bellevue, Washington. He's still making them in various sizes and colors, both as finished flies and in kits (see Materials, Tools, Rigging chapter), and they are unchanged from the 1965 original except for the addition of plastic doll's eyes. His Pop-Eyed Poppers have been used all over the world for saltwater game fish. In his 35 years of experience designing tube flies, Joe has come up with many innovations, both in fly construction, hook rigging, and the application of new materials.

Butorac's Pop-Eyed Popper

Tubing: 3" of 1/8" hard plastic tubing (Joe uses chemical laboratory tubing, which, unlike the coiled lengths of carburetor or pressure gauge tubing, is perfectly straight (see Materials, Tools, Rigging chapter) and 1" of 3/16" soft tubing.
Thread: White "A" rod winding thread.

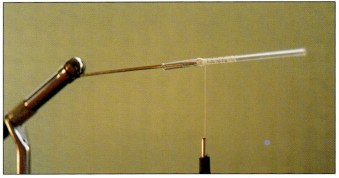

Step 1: Insert the hard tubing 1/2" into the soft tubing and put the joined sections on your vise, soft tubing end in first. Start your thread on the hard tubing and wrap it up and onto the soft tubing about 1/8", locking the sections in place. Then wrap the thread forward to 3/4 the length of the popper head you will be using.

Step 2: Rotate the tube 1/4 turn (90°)—this puts the designated "side" of the tube facing up. In this fly, the side feathers go on first. (For convenience, Joe always ties on top of the tube.) Select four 6 to 7" strung white saddle hackles. Stack the feathers with the narrowest on the inside, the widest on the outside. This gives a nice, rounded shape. Leave the marabou fluff on and tie the feathers on top of the tube with their concave sides inward.

Step 3: Select three more white saddles, all slightly broader than the first bunch. Tie in as in Step 2. (Joe separates the seven total hackles into two bunches because that way he can lock them in better with thread wraps.)

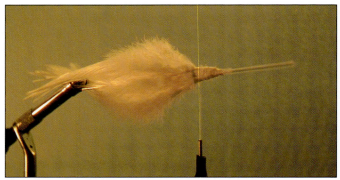

Step 4: Rotate the tube 180° and repeat Steps 2 and 3.

Step 5: Cut two 4" lengths of large pearl Mylar piping, remove the cores, and fray out 3" of their lengths with a comb. Lay one of the pieces of piping on top of the tube (the designated "side" of fly) so the frayed ends of the Mylar extend almost the length of the saddles and tie down the unfrayed end. Rotate the tube 180°.

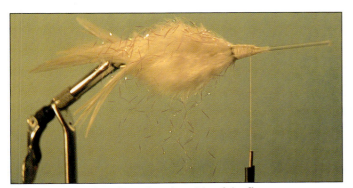

Step 6: Repeat Step 5 on the other side of the fly.

Step 7: Fray out the rest of the tied-in Mylar with a comb. Now it's time to designate the fly's "top" and "bottom". Dampen the feathers slightly with water, then rotate the fly to find their natural droop. Rotate the tube so the maximum hang down is on the fly's bottom side. Select four 6 to 7" turquoise blue strung saddle hackles. Lay them flat on top of the tube and tie them in.

Step 8: Select two more turquoise blue saddles, slightly broader than the first and tie them on top. Select one more turquoise blue saddle, slightly broader than the others (the best one) and tie it on top, dead center. Whip finish.

Step 9: Paint the dorsal side of the foam popper head with model airplane (plastic) paint. Let dry. Take two 8mm plastic doll's eyes and cut the rear posts in half. Make holes for the eyes in the sides of the popper head with a pencil point. This is shown on an unpainted popper head in the photo, but it should be done after the popper head is painted. Aqua Seal the eyes in place. Let dry.

Step 10: Make a pilot hole through the length of the popper head with a needle. With a pencil point indent the hole at the back of the head to make it large enough to take the thread wraps. Though shown on an unpainted popper head in the photo, it should be done after the popper head is painted.

Step 11: Apply Aqua Seal to the thread wraps and the back of the popper head.

Step 14: Carefully flex the feathers outward and against the back of the popper head so they pick up the Aqua Seal on their marabou butts.

Step 12: Push the head and tube dressing together so the marabou on the feathers presses into the Aqua Seal, making it all one unit.

Step 15: If you're using chemical tubing as Joe does, at this point make a score mark with a razor blade flush with the popper face and crack the excess tubing off. With other kinds of tubing you'll have to use the razor blade to cut all the way through.

Step 13: Push your bodkin all the way through the length of the popper head, slightly below dead center. Use the exposed tip of the bodkin as a guide by inserting the point inside the end of the tube. Shove the head onto the tube until its back is against the feathers.

The Finished Pop-Eyed Popper.

PATTERN SECTION INTRODUCTION

Fishing an alpine lake in Bavaria, Rudi Heger took this pike using a sinking line and his tube fly. Rudi Heger photo

When it comes to developing fly patterns, it's safe to say that none of us see things exactly the same way. This is true when we are discussing fancy, attractor dressings, such as those used for Atlantic salmon or Pacific steelhead, and when we are attempting to imitate a bait in a more realistic manner to trick striped bass or coho salmon. There is no right or wrong, just the simple reality that a dozen anglers observing the same baitfish will each tie up a slightly different pattern. Most of the resulting flies work, some perhaps a bit better than others.

The fact that no two tiers see things exactly the same, or that they may come up with different solutions to an identical challenge, is certainly demonstrated in the color plates of this book. One tier incorporates an intricate blend of materials to achieve a fly, while another finds it expedient to build a pattern that simply reflects the basic size, shape, and color of the bait it is intended to imitate. Some tiers work on developing an entirely new pattern to imitate a bait for a certain fishery, while others adapt an existing pattern; both with favorable results.

As you will see, many tried-and-true patterns, particularly those used in saltwater fishing, can be readily adapted to a tube—and have been. Garry Sandstrom of Tacoma, Washington, chose to convert the effective but rather fragile saltwater Streaker to a tube. In so doing, he worked out the problem of the peacock sword breakage and created a much more durable fly. Dan Blanton of San Jose, California, sent a couple of his Sar-Mul-Mac patterns tied on tubes. Dan has tried the tube method and understands the concept, but personally prefers his flies tied on a hook. He has discovered,

however, that others, and particularly those fishing the waters off Baja, commonly tie his Sar-Mul-Macs on tubes for both trolling and casting. Dan Lemaich, a die-hard steelheader from Camano Island, Washington, puts the popular spun marabou steelhead pattern on a tube for use in the Skagit River. He ties this in-the-round pattern (no designated top or bottom to the fly) on short pieces of tubing and, depending on the water clarity and flow, will string two, three, or even four of the little tubes together to give a steelhead something big to look at in turbid water.

Whether they represent adaptations of conventional, hook-tied flies or new and innovative patterns, all the flies in this book use the tubular platform to stretch the boundaries of what is possible in fly tying. We urge you to examine them exactly as they are dressed with regard to the individual tier's art; keeping in mind that these are only examples, that there might be other, even better ways to accomplish the same end. We also hope you will consider how the choices of specific materials, the tying techniques, or the dimensions these flies incorporate might work with a pattern you are developing, with observations you have made, with new materials you have found.

A truly generous spirit motivated all the fine tiers who contributed to this project. They agreed to share what they have learned so you could combine your experience with theirs and take what you need to revise, improve, and invent your own patterns. They did this because the process of individual expression, of shared insights, of careful refinement is how we fly tiers extend our realm.

4

ATLANTIC SALMON TUBE FLIES

Bill Hunter "tubed" this Laxa Adaldal salmon on a Phoenix fly. Bill Hunter photo

History

There have been a great many superb fly tiers in the history of fly fishing, people possessing hand-eye coordination and dexterity that most of us who dress hooks can only dream of. But tying prowess, no matter how refined, isn't nearly as important as the ability to innovate—to look at feather, fur, and tinsel and see beyond what is, to what might be. Imagination is what defines fly tying, and ultimately, fly fishing.

The ability to see something in a different way was certainly at play in England, around 1945 when a noted fly tier and tying instructor of the day, Mrs. Winnie Morawski, ensured her place in the annals of fly tying history by tying the first tube fly. Joseph Bates recorded in *Atlantic Salmon Flies and Fishing* that Mrs. Morawski worked as a fly tier for the firm of Charles Playfair and Company of Aberdeen, and that one day, while she was clearing away a clutter of turkey quills from her fly tying table, an idea came to her. She scraped the pith from a few short sections of turkey quills and strung them with treble hooks. Mrs. Morawski then began dressing these short sections of turkey quill with salmon and trout patterns in the traditional method of body, wing, and hackle.

On a visit to the Playfair Company, Dr. William Mitchell saw Morawski's turkey quill flies and suggested that she tie them on surgical tubing rather than quills. Eventually, the hook

was left outside the tube, so the tube could slide freely up the leader, away from the jaws of a salmon, trout, or pike. Because they were not crushed and torn by a fish's teeth during the course of battle, Morawksi's flies tied on tubes tended to last considerably longer than patterns tied directly onto hooks.

There was a problem in having a tube slide freely along the leader: the fly would sometimes spin in the current, causing it to ride improperly. To cure this, tying patterns *in the round* with hackle and wing spun completely around the tube became popular. Such dressings had no designated top or bottom, and displayed the same profile and appearance no matter how they were presented to the fish.

Tying tube flies in the round was largely, if not entirely, influenced by Richard Waddington, a famed salmon angler, fly tier and writer of the period. In his 1948 book, *Salmon Fishing - A New Philosophy* (Scribners) Waddington wrote, "My ideal salmon fly, however, is quite revolutionary. The shank will remain a steel bar—though were it not for the weight I should prefer something pliable like a heavy nylon strand. This will be linked with a plain loop to a small triangle (treble hook). The fly will not be dressed in the normal way. The body will be the same but the wing will disappear to be replaced with plenty of hackle, dressed all around the fly so that whichever way it is

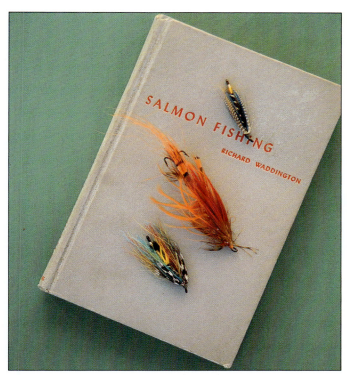

Classic salmon patterns tied on Waddington shanks by Mike Kinney. From top: Thunder and Lightning, General Practitioner, and Jock Scott. Les Johnson photo

turned it will have the same appearance." This ideal fly was tied on a wire that would become known as the Waddington Shank.

The tube fly gained popularity rapidly throughout the British Isles and Europe, being called by one British tier in the September 1959 issue of *Trout and Salmon*, "perhaps the most important advance which has occurred in salmon fly-fishing since Wood introduced the greased line method."

American fly anglers did not find the tube fly or the Waddington Shank such a revelation, in part due to angling regulations that often outlawed the use of treble hooks. All the while, anglers on the Continent continued to experiment with tube flies tied on plastic or metal tubes ranging from very short lengths to monstrous dressings up to four inches long. (The latter are still used in the strong currents of Scandinavian salmon rivers, usually with stout, two-handed rods.) British tiers cut their own tubes from empty ball-point pens, hypodermic needles, and automotive pressure gauge tubing to dress the same patterns they had always tied on hooks. During this period, traditional attractor patterns such as the Hairy Mary, Blue Charm, March Brown, Jock Scott, Black Doctor, Green Highlander, Akroyd, and others were successfully adapted to tubes with slight modifications in tying methods and materials, but aside from the commercial manufacture of plastic and metal tubes specifically for fly tying, there were few advances in tube fly design and technology. The steadily increasing interest in saltwater fly fishing in the United States would set the stage for further evolution of tube flies.

TUBE CONVERSIONS OF CLASSIC ATLANTIC SALMON FLIES

Mickey Finn

Tubing: 2" of 1/8" hard plastic tubing and a 1/2" piece of 1/8" O.D. vinyl tubing for a hook holder, or a Slipstream 2" plastic tube.
Thread: Black.

Step 1: Put the tube on your vise and attach the tying thread. 1/4" from the rear end of the tube tie in a piece of fine silver oval tinsel (the ribbing). Wrap the thread forward to 1/4" from the front end. Tie in a piece of medium flat silver tinsel. Wind the flat tinsel down the tube to the oval tinsel, then wrap it back to the head of the fly and tie it down. Rib forward with six turns of oval tinsel and tie it down. Trim the excess tinsel.

Step 2: Mix a very small bunch of red and yellow bucktail for the wings. Tie half of the mixed bucktail on the top of the tube, making the wing slightly longer than the tube.

Step 3: Rotate the tube 180° in the vise so the first wing becomes the belly of the fly. Tie the other half of the mixed bucktail on the top of the tube, and make it the same length as the first. Both sides of the body should be visible. Trim the excess bucktail.

Step 4: Make a small, neat head with black thread, whip finish, and lacquer the wraps.

Red Shrimp

Tubing: 2" of 1/8" hard plastic tubing and a 1/2" piece of 1/8" O.D. vinyl tubing for a hook holder, or a Slipstream 2" plastic tube.
Thread: Red.

Step 1: Put the tube on your vise and attach the tying thread. 1/4" from the rear end of the tube tie in a piece of fine silver oval tinsel (the ribbing). Wrap the thread forward to midbody and tie a piece of red floss. Wind red floss down to meet the oval tinsel, then back to midbody. Tie it down and trim the excess. Rib the red floss with five or six turns of oval tinsel, then tie it down, and trim the excess.

Step 2: At midbody tie in a sparse badger hackle. The hackle barbs should point to the rear, wet fly style. Wrap a few turns of hackle at the midpoint, then tie it down, and trim the excess. Directly in front of the hackle, tie in another piece of fine silver oval tinsel. Wrap the thread forward to 1/4" from the front end of the tube and tie in a length of black floss. Wind the black floss down to the hackle, then back to the thread stopping point. Tie down the floss and trim the excess. Rib the black floss with five or six turns of oval tinsel, then tie it down, and trim the excess.

Step 3: Tie a very small bunch of red bucktail on the top of the tube, making the wing slightly longer than the tube.

Step 4: Rotate the tube 180° in the vise so the first wing becomes the belly of the fly. Tie a matching amount of red bucktail on the top of the tube, and make it the same length as the first. Both sides of the body should be visible. Trim the excess bucktail.

Step 5: Make a small, neat head with red thread, whip finish, and lacquer the wraps.

Silver Doctor

Tubing: 2" of 1/8" hard plastic tubing and a 1/2" piece of 1/8" O.D. vinyl tubing for a hook holder, or a Slipstream 2" plastic tube.
Thread: Red.

Step 1: Put the tube on your vise and attach the tying thread. 1/4" from the rear end of the tube tie in a piece of fine silver oval tinsel (the ribbing). Wrap the thread forward to 1/4" from the front end and tie in a piece of medium flat silver tinsel. Wind the flat tinsel down to meet the oval tinsel, then back to the head of the fly and tie it down. Rib forward with six turns of the oval tinsel and tie it down. Trim the excess tinsel.

Step 2: Mix a very small bunch of dark red, medium blue, yellow, and black bucktail for the wings. Tie half of the mixed bucktail on the top of the tube, making the wing slightly longer than the tube.

Step 3: Rotate the tube in the vise 180° so the first wing becomes the belly of the fly. Tie the other half of the mixed bucktail on the top of the tube, and make it the same length as the first. Both sides of the body should be visible. Trim the excess bucktail.

Step 4: Make a small head, whip finish, and lacquer.

Silver Stoat

Tubing: 2" of 1/8" hard plastic tubing and a 1/2" piece of 1/8" O.D. vinyl tubing for a hook holder, or a Slipstream 2" plastic tube.
Thread: Black.

Step 1: Put the tube on your vise and attach the tying thread. 1/4" from the rear end of the tube tie in a piece of fine silver oval tinsel (the ribbing). Wrap the thread forward to 1/4" from the front end and tie in a piece of medium flat silver tinsel. Wind the flat tinsel down to meet the oval tinsel, then back to the head of the fly and tie it down. Rib forward with seven or eight turns of the oval tinsel and tie it down. Trim the excess tinsel.

Step 2: Tie a very small bunch of black bucktail on the top of the tube, making the wing slightly longer than the tube.

Step 3: Rotate the tube in the vise 180° so the first wing becomes the belly of the fly. Tie a matching amount of black bucktail on the top of the tube, and make it the same length as the first. Both sides of the body should be visible. Trim the excess bucktail.

Step 4: Make a small head, whip finish, and lacquer.

Thunder and Lightning

Tubing: 2" of 1/8" hard plastic tubing and a 1/2" piece of 1/8" O.D. vinyl tubing for a hook holder, or a Slipstream 2" plastic tube.
Thread: Black.

Step 1: Put the tube on your vise and attach the tying thread. 1/4" from the rear end of the tube tie in a piece of fine gold oval tinsel (the ribbing) and an orange saddle hackle (tip first, with the barbs pointing back, wet fly style). Wrap the thread forward to 1/4" from the front end and tie in a piece of black floss. Wind the black floss down to the tinsel, then back to the head of the fly. Tie it down, and trim the excess. Rib forward with six turns of the oval tinsel to the head, tie it down, and trim the excess. Rib forward to the head with six turns of orange hackle, tie it down, and trim the excess.

Step 2: Tie a small bunch of natural brown bucktail on the top of the tube, making the wing slightly longer than the tube.

Step 3: Rotate the tube in the vise 180° so the first wing becomes the belly of the fly. Tie a matching amount of natural brown bucktail on the top of the tube, and make it the same length as the first. Both sides of the body should be visible. Trim the excess bucktail.

Step 4: Tie in a guinea fowl feather dyed bright blue as a front hackle, wet fly style. Make a couple of turns of it, tie it down, and trim the excess. Complete the fly by making a small, neat head with black thread, whip finish, and lacquer the wraps.

Step 2: Tie a very small bunch of black bucktail on the top of the tube, making the wing slightly longer than the tube.

Step 3: Rotate the tube in the vise 180° so the first wing becomes the belly of the fly. Tie a matching amount of black bucktail on the top of the tube, and make it the same length as the first. Both sides of the body should be visible. Trim the excess bucktail.

Step 4: Make a small head, whip finish, and lacquer.

Garry Dog

Tubing: 2" of 1/8" hard plastic tubing and a 1/2" piece of 1/8" O.D. vinyl tubing for a hook holder, or a Slipstream 2" plastic tube.
Thread: Black.

Step 1: Put the tube on your vise and attach the tying thread. 1/4" from the rear end of the tube tie in a piece of fine silver oval tinsel (the ribbing). Wrap the thread forward to 1/4" from the front end and tie in a piece of black floss. Wind the black floss down to the tinsel, then back to the head of the fly. Tie it down and trim the excess. Rib forward with six turns of the oval tinsel, tie it down, and trim the excess.

Step 2: Mix a small bunch of red and yellow bucktail for the wings. Tie half the mixed bucktail on the top of the tube, making the wing slightly longer than the tube.

Step 3: Rotate the tube in the vise 180° so the first wing becomes the belly of the fly. Tie the other half of the mixed bucktail on the top of the tube, and make it the same length as the first. Both sides of the body should be visible. Trim the excess bucktail.

Step 4: Tie in a guinea fowl feather dyed bright blue as a front hackle, wet fly style. Make a couple of turns, tie it down, and trim. Complete the fly by making a small, neat head with black thread, whip finish, and lacquer the wraps.

Stoat Tail

Tubing: 2" of 1/8" hard plastic tubing and a 1/2" piece of 1/8" O.D. vinyl tubing for a hook holder, or a Slipstream 2" plastic tube.
Thread: Black.

Step 1: Put the tube on your vise and attach the tying thread. 1/4" from the rear end of the tube tie in a piece of fine silver oval tinsel (the ribbing). Wrap the thread forward to 1/4" from the front end and tie in a piece of black floss. Wind the black floss down to the tinsel, then back to the head of the fly. Tie it down and trim the excess. Rib forward with seven turns of the oval tinsel to the head, tie it down, and trim the excess.

ATLANTIC SALMON TUBE FLIES

The tube fly patterns that follow are listed under the name of their originator and/or tier.

Roland Holmberg (Stockholm, Sweden)

Roland Holmberg photo

Roland Holmberg is an Atlantic salmon guide on Norway's renowned Gaula and Aa Rivers. He has fished tube flies from Scandinavia to British Columbia, from Baja to Tierra del Fuego. In one evening, the Sea Habit tube fly produced these three Norwegian Atlantic salmon , 23 to 29 pounds for Holmberg

Sea Habit

Tubing: 1" long 1/8" aluminum tube. Also tied on up to 3" lengths of plastic, brass, or copper tubing.
Thread: 6/0 white, black.

Step 1: Put a 1" aluminum tube on your vise and attach the white tying thread at the front end. Wind the thread down to 1/2" from the front end. Wax the thread and spin white dubbing on it, then wrap the dubbing forward, creating a ball 1/4" wide. Use wraps of thread to build up the diameter of the tube right in front of the ball as a base for tying the other materials. Whip finish.

Step 2: Select two matching jungle cock feathers, coat them with Dave's Flexament and let them dry.

Step 3: Attach the black thread to the front of the tube and wind it to the start of the ball. Cut two 3 1/4" pieces of pearl Flashabou and tie them in on either side of the ball.

Step 4: Select a soft, blue saddle hackle and tie it in, wet fly style, right in front of the ball. Wind the hackle on, tie it down, and trim the excess. Spread the hackle fibers apart over the wing area, dividing them in half, then pulling them to either side and down, out of the way of the wing.

Step 5: Tie in a sparse, tapered 3 3/4" wing of natural white polar bear, goat hair, or polar bear FisHair. Trim the excess and cement. Top this with a 4 1/2" wing of turquoise blue polar bear hair, goat hair, or FisHair. The second wing should be about one-half the volume of the first. Trim the excess and cement. Top this with another sparse, tapered 3 3/4" wing of natural white polar bear, goat hair, or polar bear, the same volume as the first. Trim the excess and cement. Top this with a tapered 4" black wing that is twice the volume of the white wing. Trim the excess and cement.

Step 6: Cut two 3 1/2" pieces of light blue Krystal Flash and tie them in on either side of the tube so they both lay along the center line of the wing.

Step 7: Tie in the pair of jungle cock eyes you've prepared. Build up a neatly tapered head with black thread. Whip finish and lacquer or epoxy the wraps.

Holmberg Note: "This fly was originally developed for Atlantic salmon, fishing them fresh from the sea. The Sea Habit has given me more than 100 Atlantic salmon. It was also very good for steelhead, Mexican dorado, and even billfish."

Johnson Note: "Richard Waddington made extensive comparisons in *Salmon Fishing - A New Philosophy* between the Atlantic salmon's feeding instincts at sea and its taking of a fly in freshwater. He wrote that the salmon's sea habit of hunting for food is so deeply ingrained that it continues even after the fish enters freshwater and stops its active feeding. According to Waddington, when a salmon that has returned to its natal river sees a bait-imitating fly, three to four inches long, it reverts to the habit of its sea life and strikes. This is the premise behind Roland Holmberg's fine salmon fly—and why he named it the Sea Habit."

Bill Hunter (New Boston, New Hampshire)

Bill Hunter with a hefty Atlantic salmon done in by a tube fly on Norway's Namsen River. Bill Hunter photo

Bill Hunter has contributed many new fly patterns and modifications of old standards to the conventional list for salmon, trout, and bonefish. He regularly fishes the Florida Keys, the Rockies, Alaska, the principal Atlantic salmon rivers of the Canadian Maritime, Iceland, and Norway. He has also fished in New Zealand, Chile, Argentina, the Bahamas, Australia, Kiribati, and Panama. For the last five years he has been exploring Russia's Kamchatka and Kola Peninsulas and the mainland tundra rivers. He is a contributor to a variety of outdoor magazines, both in the U.S. and abroad. His traditional, hook-tied salmon flies appeared in Judith Dunham's, *The Atlantic Salmon Fly* (Chronicle Books, 1991). In 1975 he designed the popular HMH Fly Tying Vise, and his new tube fly tying tool is currently being manufactured by Kennebec River Fly and Tackle Co. (see Materials, Tools, Rigging chapter).

Phoenix Fly
Tied by Rod Yerger

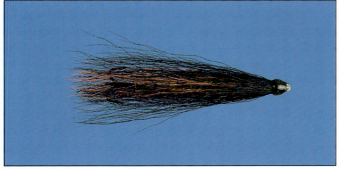

Tubing: 1/2 to 2 1/2" aluminum tube to suit the size of the fly.
Thread: Black.

Step 1: Tie in a piece of oval silver tinsel (the ribbing) at the rear of the tube. Advance the thread to the front of the tube. Tie in and wrap the tube with flat gold tinsel, down to the rib and back, then rib it with the oval silver tinsel.

Step 2: Tie in several small bunches of bucktail, black being the primary color, with sparse highlights of magenta and purple bucktail. Evenly distribute these winging materials 360° around the tube.

Step 3: Tie in a few strands of fluorescent purple Krystal Flash, evenly spaced around the tube.

Step 4: Tie in a few strands of black bucktail mixed with blue Krystal Flash and wine Krystal Flash in equal amounts, evenly distributed around the tube.

Step 5: Add a final application of black bucktail, evenly distributed around the tube.

Step 6: Whip finish the head and apply head cement.

Hunter Note: "This fly has produced well in Russia on the Ponoi, drew strikes on the Kocha and Norway's Namsen, and saved the week for my partner and I on Iceland's Laxa Adaldal in July of 1993 taking a dozen salmon."

Silver Smelt
Tied by Rod Yerger

Tubing: 1 1/2 to 2 1/2" aluminum tubing to suit the size of the fly.
Thread: White.

Step 1: Tie in a body of flat gold tinsel ribbed with oval silver tinsel.

Step 2: Tie in some white bucktail, distributed evenly, 360 degrees around the tube. The amount of white bucktail used in the wing of the Silver Smelt should be equal to the combined amount of all other winging materials.

Step 3: Tie in a few strands of pearl Krystal Flash, evenly distributed around the tube.

Step 4: Tie in a few purple and blue bucktail fibers, mixed, then evenly distributed around the tube.

Step 5: Tie in a few strands of copper Krystal Flash, evenly distributed around the tube.

Step 6: Tie in a small amount of black bucktail fibers, evenly distributed around the tube.

Step 7: Whip finish and apply head cement.

Step 8: Shoulder the fly with small jungle cock eyes, or paint yellow and black eyes on either side of the head.

Hunter Note: "This early season pattern has produced well on Russia's Ponoi, the Chorney, and landed two of my best fish on the Varzina. I suspect it will work well elsewhere."

Muom Orange
Tied by Rod Yerger

Tubing: Usually tied on a 1 1/2 to 2 1/2" aluminum tube. Also on copper for a heavier pattern suitable for big rivers in Norway.

Thread: Danville's hot orange.

Step 1: Tie in a few strands of pearl Krystal Flash for a tail.

Step 2: Tie in a tag of gold oval tinsel, leaving enough length to rib the body.

Step 3: The body is tied in two equal sections of Danville's #7 orange chenille. Between these sections, tie in a band of black chenille, followed by a hot, reddish-orange neck hackle folded and wound three turns.

Step 4: Rib with gold oval tinsel.

Step 5: Tie in a sparse, even layer of yellow bucktail, distributed 360° around the tube.

Step 6: Over the yellow bucktail, lay in a few strands of copper and pearl Krystal Flash, mixed, and slightly shorter than the yellow wing.

Step 7: Tie in a sparse layer of hot orange bucktail evenly distributed over the yellow bucktail.

Step 8: Shoulder the fly with two small jungle cock eyes set opposite one another on the tube.

Step 9: Whip finish and apply head cement.

Black Maria
Tied by Rod Yerger

Tubing: Tied on standard 1/2 to 2 1/2" Slipstream plastic or aluminum tubes. Also on copper for a heavier pattern suitable for big rivers in Norway.

Thread: Danville's black.

Step 1: Tie in a tag of gold oval tinsel, leaving enough length to rib the body.

Step 2: Tie in a body of black floss or wool yarn.

Step 3: Rib the body with oval gold tinsel.

Step 4: On top of the tube, tie in a wing made of a sparse layer of black bear hair or black dyed bucktail.

Step 5: Top the wing with two layers of Flashabou (15 strands each), red over blue.

Hunter Note: "This fly is a standard on the Alta in large dressings up to 4 inches long. It has also produced well on a variety of Russian rivers in 1 to 2 1/2" lengths. In Iceland I like the Black Maria tied on 1/2 to 1" tubes."

Tippet Shrimp
Tied by Rod Yerger

Tubing: Tied on standard 1/2 to 2 1/2" Slipstream or aluminum tubes. Also on copper for a heavier pattern suitable for big rivers in Norway.

Thread: Danville's hot orange.

Step 1: Tie in a tail of reddish-orange calf tail fibers mixed with pearl and gold Krystal Flash, 1 1/2 to 2" long.

Step 2: Tie in a tag of gold oval tinsel, leaving enough length to rib the body.

Step 3: Wrap the rear half of the body with Danville's #7 orange chenille.

Step 4: Tie in small golden pheasant tippet sections on either side of chenille. The golden pheasant tippet fibers should have unmarked fibers removed and tips cut out by snipping the stem about 5/8" down from the tip. This leaves you with V-shaped tippet sections. Tie these in on either side of the fly just ahead of the orange chenille. After tying the tippet feathers on either side of the tube, snip off the butts and carefully rotate the fibers around the tube with your thumbnail to form an even collar of tippet hackle.

Step 5: Tie in front half of body with reddish-orange sparkle dubbing, full and shaggy, picked out and ribbed with three turns of gold oval tinsel. For an optional heavier dressing, wind a folded hot orange saddle hackle through the dubbed front section of the fly following the turns of ribbed tinsel.

Step 6: Add a front collar of natural red golden pheasant body feather. Fold the feather and make three turns to complete collar.

Step 7: Whip finish and apply head cement.

Hunter Note: "This is one of the best flies of the 1993 season. Using the Tippet Shrimp I've taken fish in Russia, Canada, Iceland and Norway. This same fly tied on a standard salmon hook was the top producer for the year and took fish on both sides of Russia from Kola to Kamchatka."

Gunnar Lindbäck (Bandhagen, Sweden)

Gunnar Lindbäck combined one of his Atlantic salmon tube flies with a white foam popper head to take this 30-pound dorado. Les Johnson photo

Step 2: Select two matching jungle cock feathers, coat them with Dave's Flexament and let them dry.

Step 3: Wind the grizzly saddle hackle forward, palmer style, spacing the wraps so you get about six or seven turns to the thread starting point, 1/4" from the front end of the tube. Tie down and trim the excess. Cement.

Step 4: From a piece of black monkey skin with 3 1/2" hairs cut a 2" long, 1/8" wide strip. Tie the front end of the strip on top of the tube at the head of the fly. Secure well with thread, and cement.

Step 5: Wind the fine silver oval tinsel forward, wrapping down the monkey skin strip every 1/4", Matuka style, in six evenly spaced turns to the thread starting point. Tie down, trim the excess and cement.

Step 6: Rotate the tube 180° in the vise. On top of the tube tie in a sparse bunch of black bucktail 2 1/4" long. Trim the excess and cement.

Step 7: Rotate the tube 180° again and on top of the monkey strip, tie in six strands of 3 3/4" long peacock herl. Tie down the herl, trim the excess, and cement. On either side of the head tie in the jungle cock eyes you've prepared. Trim the butts and tie them down. Form a neatly tapered head with thread, whip finish and cement the wraps.

Lindbäck Note: Last season in Norway my best fish on the Monkey Fly were a 25-pound salmon from the Gaula and a 20-pounder from the Namsen. This fly also took a 14-pound sea trout from the River Em. I caught smaller salmon and sea trout on it as well. I mostly fish the big Monkey flies very close to the bank during high-water."

Gunnar's Monkey

Tubing: 2" of 1/8" hard plastic tubing.
Thread: Black.

Step 1: Put 2" of hard plastic tubing on your vise. Attach your thread 1/4" from the front end of the tube and wind it back to 1/8" from the rear of the tube. Tie in a piece of fine silver oval tinsel at the rear of the tube; at the same place, tie in a grizzly saddle hackle, tip first. Then advance the thread back to the head. Tie in a piece of medium silver flat tinsel, and in tight turns wrap it to the rear of the tube, then wrap it back to the front, tie down the tinsel and trim the excess. Cement.

Gunnar's Bunny

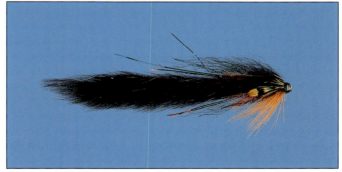

Tubing: 1/2" Slipstream copper tube.
Thread: Black.

Step 1: Attach the tying thread to the tube. In the middle of the tube, dub on a small ball of black fur or SLF.

Step 2: In front of the ball, on top of the tube tie in a sparse 3/4" long bunch of red orange SLF hank, Arctic fox tail, or calf tail.

Step 3: On top of that, tie in three or four strands each, mixed, red Flashabou and blue Flashabou, 2 1/2" long.

Step 4: On top of that, tie in a 4" long, black rabbit fur strip.

Step 5: Top the rabbit strip with a few strands each, mixed, red Flashabou Tinselflash and blue Flashabou Tinselflash, varying in length from 2 1/2 to 3 1/2". They should look ragged and uneven.

Step 6: Tie in an orange saddle hackle, wet fly style. Wrap the hackle forward to form a fairly dense collar. Tie the hackle off and trim away the excess.

Step 7: On top of the tube, tie in a tapered, 1 1/2" long, medium-sized bunch of black dyed Arctic fox, or similar hair. This should overlay and conceal the hackle on the top side of the tube and the tips of the hair should blend in with the base of the rabbit strip.

Step 8: Tie in a pair of jungle cock eyes and build a small head with black thread. Cement the wraps.

Davy Wotton (Pontypool, Gwent, Wales, U.K.)

Renowned U.K. fly tier Davy Wotton selects one of his Blue Lightning tube flies to fish this beautiful water near his home in Wales. Davy Wotton photo

Davy Wotton is arguably Britain's best known professional fly tier and is ranked as one of the world's finest. Over the years he has introduced and developed many new fishing techniques and fly patterns, and is a regular contributor to fly tying and fly fishing magazines in the U.K. and overseas.

Davy lives very close to the famous River Usk, one of the classic salmon rivers of Wales and the U.K. Over the years the Usk has given Davy a number of fish in the 20 pound class, and it remains by today's standards a very good river. The Three Salmons Hotel, which still stands on the side of the River Usk, was patronized by such great names as Kelson, Francis, Treherne, and Price Tannant—all of whom were masters of the classic salmon fly. Many of the salmon patterns known today originated in this hotel, which set aside a room with a tying vise and materials for its guests' use.

Heavy Brass Fly #1

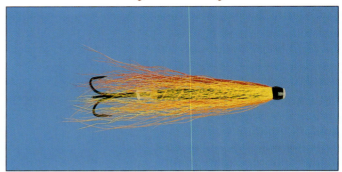

Tubing: 2 1/4" heavy brass Slipstream tube with plastic liner. A plastic liner is essential to avoid the risk of the tippet chaffing against the metal edge. On the back end of the tube is a 3/8" long extension of 1/8" I.D. clear hard plastic tubing for holding the hook eye. This extension can be made of any flexible tubular material that will go over the end of the tube and hold firm to both it and the hook eye. Often, the hook holder is soft vinyl of a suitable diameter. When the metal and plastic tubing are connected, their overall length is 2 1/2".
Thread: Black.

Step 1: Put the tube on your vise and attach the tying thread. Tie in a piece of fine gold oval tinsel on the rear plastic hook holder. Leave enough room for a tag of four or five forward turns of tinsel before it reaches the brass tube. Advance the tying thread to 1/4" from the front of the tube. At the head, tie in a long piece of black floss and then wind the floss down the body, stopping at a point that will allow four or five forward turns of the gold tinsel tag. Wind the floss back over the body to the tying thread at the front—this double layer of floss will keep the material from moving on the tube and opening up a gap (Davy uses this procedure with tinsel bodies as well). Tie down and trim the excess floss. Wrap the oval tinsel forward four or five close turns to make a tag, up to the edge of the floss, then rib forward to the head with it in six evenly spaced turns. Secure and trim the excess tinsel.

Step 2: Cut a small bunch of red bucktail for the first wing. Tie it on the top of the tube, making the wing extend an inch past the end of the plastic hook holder.

Step 3: Rotate the tube in the vise one third of a turn, so the red wing lies along the body's lower side. Tie in an equal amount of yellow bucktail on the top of the tube, and make this second wing the same length as the first. The side of the body should be visible between the two wings.

Step 4: Rotate the tube another one third of a turn, so the yellow wing lies along the body's lower side. Tie in an equal amount of orange bucktail on the top of the tube, and make this third wing the same length as the other two. The side of the body should be visible between the yellow and orange wings as well. Trim the excess bucktail.

Step 5: Make a small, neat head with black thread, whip finish, and lacquer or epoxy the wraps.

Wotton Note: "At times a large amount of material may be tied in for the wing here. In essence, too small an amount of material is generally not effective for a large fly fished at depth unless the short tube, long wing design (see Davy's Long Wing flies) is used."

Heavy Brass Fly #2

Tubing: 2 1/2" heavy brass Slipstream tube with an attached 3/4" long, flexible tubing hook holder. The overall length of connected tubing is 3".
Thread: Red, black.

Step 1: Slip a piece of medium silver Mylar piping over the tube, so about 3/8" of piping extends past the rear end of the brass tube. Tie down the Mylar 1/8" from the end of the brass tube with a few turns of red thread, whip finish and lacquer the thread.

Step 2: Using black thread, tie down the other end of the Mylar piping a little more than 1/4" from the front of the tube. Trim away the excess piping. Cut a sparse bunch of yellow bucktail and tie it on top of the tube. Make the wing extend an inch past the end of the brass tube.

Step 3: Rotate the vise one quarter turn so the yellow wing is aligned with the side of the fly. Cut a sparse bunch of black bucktail and tie it in on top of the tube, same length as yellow wing. Rotate the vise one quarter turn so the black wing is aligned with the side of the fly. Repeat this procedure with another yellow and another black wing. All four wings should be so sparse that the sides of the body show through beneath them. Trim the excess bucktail. Form a small, neat head with black thread that ends 1/8" from the front of the tube. Whip finish and lacquer the wraps. Let dry.

Step 4: Using red thread, tie in a guinea fowl feather dyed bright blue in front of the black head. Wind the feather a couple of

turns, wet fly style, then tie down and trim. Form a small, neat head with red thread. Whip finish and lacquer or epoxy the wraps.

Wotton Note: "Flies tied on heavy brass tubes like these are generally used in early season (in the U.K.) when fish lie deep in heavy water and will not rise to the surface due to the water temperature. They are also used on waters that do not allow spinning methods. These patterns demand powerful rods and heavy 11 and 12 weight lines."

Long Wing Orange

Tubing: 1/8" plastic or brass or aluminum tubes of varying lengths. Example shown is plastic, 5/8" in length, with a 5/8" long, flexible tubing hook holder attached. The overall length of the connected tubes is 1".
Thread: Orange.

Step 1: Tie in sparse 4" wing of orange dyed goat (or hair from the back leg of a collie dog, or Arctic fox) on top of tube, 3/16" from the front end of the tube. Trim the excess.

Step 2: Ahead of the wing, tie in a soft orange hackle and wrap a couple of turns, wet fly style. Tie it down and trim the excess.

Step 3: Tie in jungle cock feathers on either side of the wing. Trim away hackle butts. Make a small, neat head with orange thread. Whip finish. Lacquer or epoxy the wraps.

Long Wing Red and Black

Tubing: 1/8" plastic, or brass or aluminum tubes of varying lengths. Example shown is aluminum, 1 1/2" in length, with a 3/8" long flexible tubing hook holder attached. The overall length of the connected tubes is 1 3/4".
Thread: Black.

Step 1: Put tube on your vise and attach the tying thread. 3/16" from the front end of the tube tie in a piece of red floss. Wind the floss down the body to the edge of the hook holder, then wind it back to the tying thread at the front. Tie the floss down and trim the excess. Tie in fine silver embossed tinsel at the head and rib down the body to the hook holder, then back up the body to the head, crisscrossing the first rib as you go. Tie down the tinsel and trim the excess.

Step 2: Tie in a sparse 4" wing of black goat (or hair from the back leg of a collie dog or Arctic fox). Trim the excess.

Step 3: Make a small, neat head with black thread. Whip finish and lacquer or epoxy the wraps.

Long Wing Black

Tubing: 1/8" plastic, or brass or aluminum tubes of varying lengths. Example shown is plastic 1" in length, with a 3/4" long, flexible tubing hook holder attached. The overall length of the connected tubes is 1 1/2".
Thread: Black.

Step 1: Tie in a sparse 4" wing of black goat (or hair from the back leg of a collie dog or Arctic fox) 3/16" from the front end of tube. Trim the excess. Make a small, neat head from black thread. Whip finish and lacquer or epoxy the wraps.

Wotton Note: "Long wing lures have become very popular in the U.K. They are fished at all depths but are generally used in fast, streamy water, which of course provides mobility to the long wing of the fly. Probably the best known of these flies is the Collie Dog. Hair from the back leg of the dog is used for the wing, though goat is just as good. Many variants of course have now come about. The sample fly with the red body and black wing has actually caught five fish."

Dapping Tube

Tubing: 1/8" hard plastic, 1" in length with 3/8" long, flexible tubing hook holder attached The overall length of the connected tubes is 1 1/2".
Thread: Red.

Step 1: 1/8" from the rear end of the plastic tube tie in a piece of extra fine silver oval tinsel. Make a dubbing loop and spin purple SLF (see "Materials, Tools, Rigging" chapter) dubbing onto it. Advance the thread to 1/8" from the front of the tube. Wind the purple dubbing forward to the thread, tie it down and trim the excess. At the head, tie in a long, black dry fly hackle, butt first. Palmer the body with the hackle, winding it down to the tail end. (Davy says palmering from front to back like this gives the hackle points a steep, almost 90° angle, which is desirable in this type of fly.) Maintaining tension on the hackle tip, bring the ribbing tinsel up through it to bind it down. Rib up to the thread at the head. This should be done quickly, rather than slowly and deliberately, so as not to trap the hackle fibers. Tie down the tinsel. Trim the excess hackle, fore and aft, and the excess tinsel.

Step 2: Tie in guinea fowl feather dyed red. Wind several turns, wet fly style, tie it down and trim the excess.

Step 3: Make small, neat head with red thread. Whip finish and lacquer or epoxy the wraps.

Wotton Note: "This is a tube version of a dapping fly. This style of fly is mostly used for salmon and sea trout fished for on the lakes and lochs that they venture into after running the river system that flows into or out of the loch. There are basically two methods to fish this style. The first is with the use of a longish rod and a blowline: the dapped fly is allowed to trip the water surface in front of the boat which is drifting downwind. You need to have a good blow for this method but it can provide thrilling results. In the second, more traditional method a rod of around ten feet is used. On the tail of the cast (the end of the leader) is tied a small single hook fly or tube. Above this (three to six feet) is tied a dropper, and the dapping fly is tied onto this. The flies are worked in such a way as to induce the fish to rise to the surface and take one or the other of the flies. Usually the bushy top fly is taken with a flurry of water as the fish takes and turns down with the fly. Great fun!"

Yellow Dolly Muddler
Tube pattern by Hugh Falkus
Tied by Davy Wotton

Tubing: 1/8" plastic, 3/4" long.
Thread: White.

Step 1: Attach the thread 3/8" from the rear of tube. At that point spin a bunch of yellow deer hair on the tube. (If you have trouble doing this, Davy suggests using a hair stacker to first align the tips of a bunch of cut deer hair. Using your left hand push the bunch of hair over the tube, surrounding it, then with your right hand take two turns of thread over the hair and tube. When you draw the thread tight, it will flare out around the tube.) Compress and lock the hair with several turns of thread in front. Clip the yellow deer hair to 1/2" length around the tube.

Step 2: Spin a bunch of natural brown deer hair in front of the clipped yellow so the pointed tips of the brown extend just past the blunt ends of the yellow. Compress, then lock with thread. If you don't have 1/4" of brown hair in front of the yellow, spin more brown on until you do. Compress, then whip finish and lacquer the thread.

Step 3: Clip the brown hair into a muddler head, leaving the fringe of pointed brown tips over the yellow.

Wotton Note: "This fly pattern was devised by Hugh Falkus. It may be made from squirrel or deer hair. This small fly is often used for the summer grilse and for fish lying in water with a broken surface. Good after a spate (sudden) run off. Well greased, it is fished as a dry fly with a very small treble hook. I personally have used this pattern to good effect as the top dropper (see Wotton's Note: Dapping Tube) for salmon and sea trout."

Small Tubes

Tubing: Very short lengths of very small diameter plastic tube. Example is 1/16" O.D. and 1/4" long.
Thread: Black.

Step 1: A very sparse bunch of black squirrel, bear, Arctic fox (or badger, if legal) hair is tied down 1/8" from front of tube, making a wing about 1" long, and spread so as to completely encircle the tube.

Step 2: Make a small, neat head with black thread. Whip finish and lacquer the wraps. The example shown is dressed as Davy prefers, with a small red plastic spacer bead strung between the end of the tube and the hook eye. He also uses glass or plastic beads of other colors: yellow, silver, etc.

Wotton Note: "Tiny tubes with the smallest amount of hair or feather fiber are favoured for both salmon and sea trout, particularly in low water and difficult situations. At times it is the only way you will get a fish to move to the fly. Overall, black is a good color. Trout rods are often used as opposed to the double-handed salmon rods. Often you will be fishing very small waters and your concealment from the fish is of utmost importance."

SLF Prawn

This fly calls for both types of SLF: dubbing and hanks. See Materials, Tools, Rigging chapter.

Tubing: 2" Slipstream hard plastic tube and a 1/2" long, flexible tubing hook holder.
Thread: Danville orange 6/0.

Step 1: Heat the ends of two 2" lengths of 50-pound monofilament with a match. As they melt, flatten the ends. Slip onto each a small (about 3mm) black glass bead (available at sewing/fabric stores) and secure the beads at the flattened ends with a dab of Super Glue.

Step 2: Fix the hard plastic tube in your vise and start the thread 1/4" from the front end and wrap down the tube to a point 1/4" from the back end. Tie in a small bunch of orange bucktail or goat hair, making sure that it is evenly spread. It should extend 2" from the rear thread point. Bind the butts of the hair down against the tube, wrapping back to 1/4" from the front end of the tube in close turns.

Step 3: Rotate the tube 180° on the vise and wind the thread back down to the rear thread point. On top of the tube, tie in a sparse bunch of orange SLF hank fiber so that it faces back over the already tied-in hair. It should extend about 1" from the rear thread point.

Step 4: Strip all the fibers from a pair of orange hackle feathers to leave clean stems. Secure the stem butts along the sides of the tube so they point slightly upward and curve outward, and so the tips extend 2 1/2" from the rear thread point.

Step 5: With pliers flatten the mono ends of the glass bead eye stalks, then tie them along the side of the tube, so the eyes stick out 5/16" past the rear thread point. Wind the thread back to 1/4" from the front end of the tube.

Step 6: Cut a 1/4" wide strip from a sheet of red or orange Flexibody (see "Materials, Tools, Rigging" chapter) or a polyethylene plastic bag and trim one end of the strip into a tapered point. Place the strip on top of the tube, adjusting it so the tapered tip extends past the rear thread point about the same length as the eyes, then tie the strip in, making sure that it folds down equally on either side of the tube. To make it secure, use about ten close turns of thread, working towards the front of the tube. Then fold the strip of plastic back onto itself, so the untapered end overhangs the rear (eye-end) of the tube. When you double back the strip leave 1/8" of plastic forward of the last of the ten wraps of thread. Then tie the strip down onto itself and the tube, working the thread back to the rear thread point.

Step 7: Wind the thread to the middle of the tube and rotate the tube 180° in the vise. Tie in a ten inch length of six-pound monofilament on top of the tube. Loop the tag end of the mono and bind it down as well. Use enough turns to make the mono ribbing very secure.

Step 8: (For the next two steps, Davy uses a dubbing twister and recommends the Darrell Martin whirl.) Rotate the tube 180° in your vise. With the thread about 3/8" from the front end of the tube, form a dubbing loop. Move your thread half way down the shank. Place the orange SLF or seal fur dubbing into the loop and spin it into a rope. Note that the dubbing should not be spun too tightly for this fly. A good proportion of the spun material should flare away from the central core, to give the effect of legs and the bulk of the body. Wind the rope in close, touching turns towards the rear of the tube. You may have to repeat this two or three times to complete the body. The effect should be neat and chenille-like. When you're done, the thread should be at the rearmost thread position, 1/4" from the back end of the tube.

Step 9: From the orange SLF hank, cut off a section about as thick as a ballpoint pen. Flatten it out on your bench and grip the ends of the inch-wide strip with a bulldog type paper clip. Form a dubbing loop, and wind the thread to the front of the tube. Insert the bulldog-clipped SLF into the open loop so 1/4" sticks out on one side and 1" on the other. Remove the clip and spin the loop, flaring the SLF like a hackle. When the SLF is spun for the legs it is important to draw the tension down as the whirl (dubbing twister) is twisting. This will cause the SLF to flare out at a right angle and not twist around the thread. Wind the loop to 1/4" from the front end of the tube. There, secure the loop. Divide the flared fibers sticking up from the back of the fly equally on either side of the spine of the tube. Draw these fibers down so they fall on the underside of the tube. If you find this difficult, trim off the upward fibers instead.

Step 10: Fold the Flexibody or polyethylene strip forward over the body, bringing it down under great tension. Tie it down

very tightly 1/4" from the front end of the tube (tail end of the prawn). Rib the body and shellback with eight or so turns of the six-pound mono. Use the point of your dubbing needle to part the fibers, and then follow the needle point with the ribbing. Tie off and trim the surplus. Whip finish.

Step 11: At the front end of the tube cut off the excess plastic strip, making the tail section of the shellback extend 1/4" past the end of the tube. Trim the SLF legs into a tapered shape. Coating the plastic back with 5-minute epoxy glue is optional. Slip a 1/2" long flexible tubing hook holder onto eye-end of tube.

Wotton Note: "The natural prawn and shrimp are often used as bait here in the U.K. They are caught commercially, then dyed, usually red-orange or purple, and packed in an airtight bag with salt, ready for use. Natural prawns are fished on a special mount that keeps the bait straight, with a treble hook at the head end. Some waters now ban the use of the natural, but will allow an artificial. This pattern is a tube version of the SLF Prawn I originated and is also tied in purple. Though the sample here is intended for salmon, this fly can be tied in much smaller, shrimpy sizes as well."

Blue Lightning

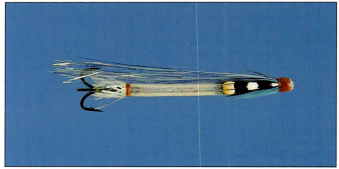

Tubing: 1/8" plastic tubing, 2" long. Keyhole one end of tube to accomodate hook eye.
Thread: Red.

Step 1: Slip medium pearl Mylar piping over tube. Extend tips of piping 3/8" past rear end of tube. Tie down piping behind flare with several turns of red thread. Whip finish and lacquer the thread.

Step 2: Tie down the piping 1/4" from the front end of the tube. Tie in a soft, kingfisher blue hackle, and wind it once, wet fly style, around the tube. Tie down and trim the excess.

Step 3: On top of the tube tie a sparse 2 3/4" wing of fine pearl purple Flashabou. It should extend past the tips of the Mylar piping about 1/2". (For a heavy dressed version of this fly, dyed blue goat hair or Arctic fox may be mixed with the Flashabou to make the wing.)

Step 4: Make a small, neat head with red thread. Whip finish and lacquer or epoxy the wraps.

Wotton Note: "This is a typical pattern that is good for the large sea trout but will also take salmon. Sea trout feed offshore on sand eels, as do salmon around some of the west coast islands off Scotland. This pattern, which I originally devised some ten years ago, has taken fish in such places. My Ghillie named it Blue Lightning, for at the time it took sea trout out of water I was fishing very quickly indeed, and has proven to be a very effective pattern. I also produce a version with a gold yellow-colored wing and hackle."

Davy's Flexbody Tube Fly

Tubing: The modular wing is tied on 1/4" of 1/8" hard plastic tubing.

Thread: Red.

Step 1: Cut a 6" piece of mono or braided mono and fold it into a 3" loop. (The loop should be about 1/2" longer than the body you intend to make.) Secure the ends of the loop to the shank of a treble or double hook (sized to suit—14, 12, 10, 8) with thread and cement.

Step 2: Slip 2 1/2" of silver Mylar tubing down over the loop and secure it at the tail end by tying it against the hook shank with thread. Whip finish and cement. Then tie the Mylar down against the mono or braid at the head end with thread, whip finish, and cement.

Step 3: Cut 1/4" of 1/8" plastic tubing. The hole in the tubing should not fit over the Mylar body, but the loop of mono or braid should pass through it. Put the tube in your vise. Tie a sparse wing of blue bucktail to the top side of the tube with red thread. Rotate the tube so this first wing is on the bottom and tie another sparse wing on the top, whip finish, and lacquer the wraps. The wings also may be tied directly onto the Mylar body.

Wotton Note: "If you tie the short tubes in Step 3 with different colors of bucktail you can quickly change wing color as needed. Body lengths from one to four inches may also be made up in advance. Small muddler heads (like the Yellow Dolly shown) are sometimes slipped onto the leader before the wing and tube are tied on. Mylar bodies of different colors may also be used. The fly can be made to spin in the water if the body of the fly is compressed toward the hook—if this is done, you must use a swivel on the leader. I originally tied up these patterns for deep water fishing from a boat for very large brown and rainbow trout found in our large (U.K.) reservoirs. I prefer to use smallish trebles—12, 14, 16—on this fly. Because the body is so flexible, it bends around in a fish's mouth and provides no leverage to work against the hold of a small hook. Small hooks provide efficient hooking power!"

Standard Dressing

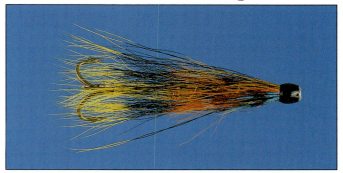

Tubing: Tied on 1/8" plastic tubing 1/2" to 1 1/2" long. Example is on a 1 1/4" plastic tube with a 1/2" long, flexible tubing hook holder. The overall length of connected tubes is 1 1/2".

Thread: Black.

Step 1: 3/16" from the rear end of the hard tube, tie in a piece of extra fine silver oval tinsel. Wrap the thread to 3/16" from the front end of the tube. Tie in a piece of black floss at the thread point. Wind the floss down the body to the hook holder, leaving room for six or seven forward turns of oval tinsel. Wind the floss back to the thread point at the head. Tie down and trim the excess floss. Wind the oval tinsel forward six or seven turns to make a tag, up to the edge of the floss, then rib forward to the head with it in six evenly spaced turns. Secure and trim the excess tinsel.

Step 2: Tie in a sparse 1 3/4" wing of gray squirrel hair dyed bright yellow. The tips should extend past the end of the hard tube about 3/4". Rotate the tube so this wing becomes the belly of the fly. Tie in an equal amount and length of the same dyed brown squirrel hair on top of the tube. Trim the excess hair.

Step 3: On top of the squirrel hair, tie in a sparse 1" topping of dyed orange Arctic fox. Rotate the tube and tie the same topping on the other wing. Tie a sparse 1/2" tuft of guinea fowl feather dyed blue on top of the orange. Rotate the tube and tie a matching tuft on top of the other bunch of orange hair. Trim away the excess hair and feather.

Step 4: Make a small, neat head with black thread. Whip finish and lacquer or epoxy the wraps.

Deer Hair Bomb

Tubing: 1 3/4" of 1/8" hard plastic tubing.

Thread: White.

Step 1: Cut 1 3/4" of plastic tubing. Put the tube in your vise. Starting 1/2" from the back end of the tube, spin on enough dark brown deer hair to make a tightly packed band 1/2" wide. Cement the wraps. Spin on an equal amount of yellow deer hair, pack it tightly, and cement the wraps. This is followed by an equal amount of tightly packed chartreuse or light green deer hair. Whip finish and cement the wraps.

Step 2: Trim the deer hair into a fat bomb shape.

Step 3: Tie a guinea fowl feather dyed bright green at the head end of the fly and wind on a couple of turns of hackle. Trim excess hackle, whip finish, and lacquer.

Wotton Note: "Based on the surface type bomber patterns, this fly is fished either on a very short leader with a fast sinking fly line, or used with a spinning rod and a lead weight attached a foot or two back from the fly. It is fished close along the bottom of the river."

Plushille Tube Fly

Tubing: 2" long, 1/8" diameter copper or aluminum Slipstream tube, with a 1" long, flexible tubing hook holder slipped over the end of the copper tube 3/8".

Thread: White.

Step 1: Put the copper or aluminum tube in your vise. Starting 3/8" from the back end of the tube, tie in the white Plushille material. Advance the thread to 3/8" from the head end of the tube. Wind forward the Plushille as a chenille. Stop 3/8" from the head end of tube, tie in 6mm glass eyes and cement the wraps. Advance the thread to 1/8" from the head end of the tube, then wind the Plushille forward to the thread point. Tie down and trim the excess Plushille, whip finish and lacquer the wraps.

Step 2: Clip the Plushille as you would deer hair, to the required shape. The example shown leaves 1" long fibers on top and bottom to form a tail. The overall length of the fly, nose to tail, is 2 3/4".

Step 3: Brush out the material well, then use waterproof markers to color the fly like a baitfish: dark back, lighter belly. Note the banded effect on back and tail of the example.

Wotton Note: "Plushille is a material developed by my friend Roman Moser. It will not float so it is suited to subsurface applications. In my experience of sea trout this fly will catch fish; I have no doubt it will also do for salmon."

Rod Yerger (Lawrence, Pennsylvania)

Rod Yerger photo

Rod Yerger is a self-taught professional fly tier. He ties flies year-round, six or seven days a week, 8 to 14 hours a day. His trout flies have appeared in numerous magazine articles, and in Eric Leiser's *Book of Fly Patterns* (Knopf, 1987), Stewart and Allen's *Flies for Trout*, Harry Murray's *Fly Fishing for Smallmouth Bass* (Lyons & Burford, 1989) and C. Boyd Pfeiffer's *Bugmaking*. (Lyons & Burford, 1993). He was primarily interested in trout patterns until 10 years ago, when he caught his first salmon on the fly on the Miramichi. At about the same time, a group of anglers from Pittsburgh who annually fish the Tweed asked if he could reproduce the Atlantic salmon tube patterns they had brought back from the U.K. He did, and the news got out, mainly by word of mouth. Now, 90 percent of his tying is for Atlantic salmon, and 60 percent of that is tube flies. Yerger believes he ties more Atlantic salmon tubes than any other professional tier on this side of the Atlantic. His clientele spends many weeks a year fishing the world's finest and most exclusive salmon rivers, so his flies get thoroughly tested.

The Bill Hunter-designed Atlantic salmon tube fly patterns shown in this book were all tied to his specifications by Rod Yerger. Yerger also contributed several patterns of his own, as well as others that he gets a lot of call for from his salmon-fishing customers. In tying tube flies, Yerger utilizes a variety of tube materials and has developed techniques can help every tier. He included the following tying notes with his selection of flies:

"I use Slipstream tubes from Veniard's in aluminum and copper, and Slipstream plastic tubes only for my Skitter tubes. I employ Papermate pen refills for most of my plastic tubes, which I purchase by the hundreds, or a case at a time. I buy them in cases of 48 cards (96 refills). Two suppliers that sell the refills in case lots are Office Depot (96 refill lots) and Office Max (48 refill lots). I usually get two to three flies from one refill. In these I place the same plastic liners used in the aluminum and copper tubes. Also, I am not content with the way the liners are melted on the aluminum and copper tubes so I purchase only the longest sizes and cut and finish them myself.

"I make my own hook sleeves—they are the result of years of experimentation. I've achieved a tapered sleeve that holds the hook securely yet allows the hook to pivot in a fish and usually work loose from the sleeve during the battle. This, of course, saves wear and tear on the fly. To achieve these results I had to decide upon a hook to use and then make the sleeves fit the hook. I use Partridge outpoint trebles on all but the Alta-style tubes on which I use Partridge Rob Wilson XX strong trebles. This system has worked well and all my customers want them only this way. The sleeves are vinyl tubing formed over a mandrel, heated and quenched so they will retain the desired shape.

"I tie my bodies differently than most I've seen from Europe. I tie the hook sleeve to the tube. Then, I build the entire body diameter up with floss to the diameter of the sleeve and put the finish body materials over.

"For the wing, I even the hair tips slightly by hand but never use a stacker. Stacked wings look great in the vise but more like a paint brush in the water.

"I tie my tube flies for fishing. Next to the ability to attract salmon, durability is the key. I lacquer all floss bodies, tinsel tips and ribs. I don't skimp on thread wraps for tying in wings, even if it means a slightly larger head. Also, I use lots of lacquer during the application of the wing materials."

Willie Gunn
Traditional pattern by Willie Gunn, riverkeeper on the River Brora (Sutherland Estates, Scotland, U.K.).
Tied by Rod Yerger

Tubing: Most commonly dressed on 1/2 to 2 1/2" aluminum or copper tubes. Can be tied on Slipstream plastic tubes or 1/8" hard plastic tubing as well.
Thread: Danville black.

Step 1: Tie in and wrap a tag of medium oval silver tinsel, leaving enough length to rib the body. Also tie in a rib of medium flat silver tinsel.

Step 2: Build an even, untapered body of black floss or wool.

Step 3: Rib the body with medium flat silver tinsel. Rib forward with small oval silver tinsel, placing the turns against the rear edge of the flat tinsel.

Step 4: Mix strands of red, yellow and black bucktail in the proportions: one part each red and yellow to one part black. Mix in a few strands of copper and gold Krystal Flash to the wing for a bit of added flash. All this winging material is distributed evenly, 360° around the tube.

Step 5: Add a sparse collar of blue dyed guinea fowl (optional).

Step 6: Whip finish and apply head cement.

Yerger Note: "This is possibly the most used tube pattern for Atlantic salmon. The standard advice one hears for selecting patterns for the Tweed and other U.K. rivers is, 'you need three flies: a Willie Gunn, a Willie Gunn, and lastly, a Willie Gunn.' This is one of the first tube patterns I tied and early on made them—according to Scottish ghillies—too bright. I was mixing the hair evenly. I later learned the way the Willie Gunn works best is to layer the hair. First a layer of mixed yellow and red covered with a layer of black. When tied this way, when the fly is wet the bright colors appear mostly at the tail. The effectiveness of this pattern—and the durability of tube flies—is illustrated by the fact that a customer of mine recently caught 31 salmon on one Willie Gunn on the Ponoi, before losing the fly to a sea trout."

General Practitioner
Traditional pattern by Esmond Drury
Tied by Ron Yerger

Tubing: Commonly dressed on aluminum tubes 1 1/2 to 2" long.
Thread: Danville red.

Step 1: For the antennae, at the rear of the tube tie in a sparse bunch of hot orange bucktail veiled top and bottom by small, natural red golden pheasant body feathers. Tie in an orange hackle, tip first, for palmering the body.

Step 2: For the body, use a dubbing of orange fur. Secure the dubbing half way up the body.

Step 3: Palmer orange hackle forward over rear half of body and secure, but do not trim. At this point, tie in natural red pheasant feathers as a base of the eyes.

Step 4: For the eyes, on top of the tube tie in a golden pheasant tippet feather with a V cut from the center and lacquered.

Step 5: Complete the dubbing and palmering of the body. Cut the palmered hackle from top of fly.

Step 6: The shellback is made of three natural red, golden pheasant body feathers. The first covers the rear half of the body; the second is longer, covering entire body; the top feather is shorter, covering half of second feather.

Step 7: Whip finish and apply head cement.

Yerger Note: "This is the classic Esmond Drury prawn pattern. When I tie these on tubes I put the shellback on the top and bottom creating a bulkier fly. Bill Hunter usually has me put eyes on the bottom of the flies I dress for him. On my own General Practitioners, I usually put eyes only on top."

Ally's Shrimp
Traditional pattern by Alistair Gowans
Tied by Rod Yerger

Tubing: Dressed on aluminum tubing 1 1/2" long. When dressed on copper tubing, 1" is the standard length.
Thread: Danville red.

Step 1: Tie in a tail of long, sparse orange bucktail.

Step 2: Tie in oval gold tinsel, for the rib.

Step 3: Wrap the rear half of body with orange floss; the front half with black floss.

Step 4: Rib the body with oval gold tinsel.

Step 5: Tie in wing of gray squirrel with golden pheasant tippet on top, flat.

Step 6: Spin on a collar of orange hackle.

Step 7: Whip finish and apply head cement.

Yerger Note: "This pattern was devised by Alistair Gowans in the early 1980s to fish the Tweed, Dee, and Tay, and was originally tied on double hooks. It was promoted as a tube to my customers by sculptor Joel Shapiro, who has used it successfully on the Alta in Norway. It has taken fish in Russia as well. I've also tied the pattern on plastic tubes for use on Quebec's Grand Cascapedia where it should be a good producer through the month of June."

Francis Fly
Traditional pattern by Peter Dean
Tied by Rod Yerger

Tubing: Usually tied on 1 1/2 to 2" aluminum or copper tubes.
Thread: Danville orange.

Step 1: Antennae: Tie in six stripped brown hackle stems (3" long) and a bunch of pheasant tail fibers.

Step 2: Tie in a pair of black round head pins for eyes.

Step 3: Tie in oval gold tinsel, for a rib.

Step 4: Build up a body with red fur dubbing or wool, large at the back, wrapped around eyes and tapering toward the front of the fly.

Step 5: Rib forward with oval gold tinsel.

Step 6: Hackle with brown saddle and trim off the top.

Step 7: Build an egg sack of orange fur dubbing or wool.

Step 8: Whip finish and apply head cement.

Yerger Note: "This is the tube version of Peter Dean's 'must' fly for Iceland. This fly has also taken salmon in Russia, Norway and the United Kingdom. Most are tied on aluminum, some on copper; 1 1/2 to 2" are standard. I substitute Dean's tied-on bead eyes with round head pins bent and tied to the tube. Red is the original color but it is just as good in orange, green, black and brown."

Comet
A ghillie's pattern, exact origin unknown
Tied by Rod Yerger

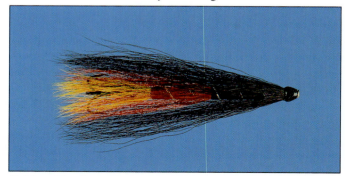

Tubing: The Comet is tied primarily on copper tubing 1/2 to 3"
Aluminum tubing is used for a lighter version.
Thread: Danville black.

Step 1: Tie in yellow bucktail distributed evenly, 360° around the tube.

Step 2: Tie in oval silver tinsel, for a rib.

Step 3: Tie in and wrap red floss to the middle of the tube, then tie off and trim excess. Build a body of floss—the rear half is red, the front half is black.

Step 4: Tie in a midwing of red bucktail at the front of the red floss, distributed evenly, 360° around the tube.

Step 5: Build the front half of the body with black floss.

Step 6: Rib forward with oval silver tinsel.

Step 7: Tie in a wing of black bucktail ahead of the black floss, distributed evenly, 360° around tube.

Step 8: Whip finish and apply head cement.

Yerger Note: "This is another of the standards. I like it best on a copper tube as it is an excellent deep pattern. The Comet can, however, be effective in slower flows or shallower water when dressed on an aluminum tube."

Alta March Brown

Tubing: Most commonly tied on an aluminum tube to match the size of the fly desired, but on a copper tube if more weight is needed.

Thread: Brown.

Step 1: Build a short tag using ten wraps of oval gold tinsel, leaving enough length to rib the body.

Step 2: Wrap body with rusty brown fur dubbing.

Step 3: Rib forward with five wraps of oval gold tinsel.

Step 4: Tie in an underwing of brown bucktail.

Step 5: Tie in an overwing of brown goat hair.

Step 6: Top the wing with several strands of peacock herl.

Step 7: Add jungle cock eyes.

Step 8: Whip finish the head and secure with cement.

Yerger Note: "Goat hair tube flies are the most productive patterns for Norway's big fish rivers—the Alta, Namsen, etc. Tubes of this style have been tied by Norwegian guides for a few years. Refinement and specific patterns I tie are the result of testing by W. Thorpe McKenzie who is an acknowledged salmon expert. Not many are able to fish the Alta, but I supply flies to those who do. The keys are the long, thick dark wing and eyes of some sort, either jungle cock or painted. All who can afford to fish the Alta opt for jungle cock. Most are dressed on aluminum tubing, some on copper. Tying in a short underwing of bucktail acts to reduce the longer goat hair's tendency to twist and snarl."

Black Sheep
Traditional pattern by Joe Hubert
(Duluth, Minnesota)
Tied by Rod Yerger

Tubing: A 1/2 to 2 1/2" aluminum tube is standard.

Thread: Black for all steps, except for the tying off of the head which is done in red.

Step 1: Tie in a tip of oval silver tinsel.

Step 2: Wrap a body of black floss.

Step 3: Tie in a bright blue hackle, short, as a beard.

Step 4: On top of the tube, tie in a bottom wing of black bucktail, followed by a midwing of yellow bucktail, followed by a top wing of black bucktail.

Step 5: Add cheeks of small jungle cock, on each side of wing.

Step 6: Finish the head with red thread and cement.

Yerger Note: "This is a tube version of the most popular of Joe Hubert's Sheep series. These flies imitate elvers, small eels that live in American and British rivers and a staple in the salmon's diet. It is always tied with jungle cock eyes which are considered essential."

Sun Ray Shadow
Pattern by an unidentified Icelandic guide
Tied by Rod Yerger

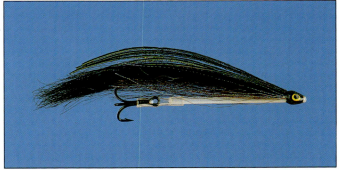

Tubing: Slipstream or Papermate pen plastic refill liner, 2 1/2 to 3" long.

Thread: Black.

Step 1: Tie in an underwing of brown bucktail, sparse and slightly longer than the tube.

Step 2: Tie in an overwing of brown goat hair, sparse and slightly longer than the bucktail.

Step 3: Tie in several strands of peacock herl as topping.

Step 4: Tie in a few strands of pearl Krystal Flash on either side of the fly. They should be the combined length of the tube and hook.

Step 5: Paint eyes, yellow with black pupil.

Step 6: Whip finish and apply head cement.

Yerger Note: "This is a goat hair pattern that has been around since the 1970s, and is used in Iceland and Norway to imitate elvers. As far as I know it was a guide's pattern that found its way into European tackle shops. It is now a standard that accounts for many salmon each season. The Sun Ray Shadow differs from other Alta patterns in three ways: the wing is usually tied more sleek; eyes are almost always painted; and since there are no body materials it is almost always dressed on a plastic tube."

Quaker Fly

Tubing: A 1 1/2 to 2 1/2" aluminum tube is standard.
Thread: Black.

Step 1: Tie in a tip of oval gold tinsel, leaving enough length to rib the body.

Step 2: Wrap a body of blue-dyed fur dubbing or wool.

Step 3: Rib the body with oval gold tinsel.

Step 4: Tie in a short hackle of red-dyed guinea, as a beard.

Step 5: Tie in a wing of blue bucktail.

Step 6: Add a topping of rainbow and red Flashabou.

Step 7: Add jungle cock eyes on either side of wing.

Yerger Note: "This pattern is rapidly gaining popularity. I first tied it at the request of experienced Atlantic salmon angler, Bill Young, using the red and blue colors of his alma mater, the University of Pennsylvania, which are colors the salmon seem to prefer. Bill has had productive fishing with it in Iceland and Norway. The name comes from Penn's mascot, the Quaker. I've tied a lot of these for my customers the past couple of years."

Beauly Snow Fly
Traditional pattern by Mr. Snowie
(Inverness, Scotland, U.K.)
Tied by Rod Yerger

Tubing: Usually dressed on 2 to 2 1/2" aluminum or copper tubes.
Thread: Black.

Step 1: Tie in a tip of oval silver tinsel. Also tie in flat silver tinsel and oval gold tinsel, for the rib.

Step 2: Wrap a body of blue fur dubbing.

Step 3: Rib forward with silver flat tinsel, followed by oval gold tinsel which should be wound to lay against the rear edge of the flat silver.

Step 4: Tie in a hackle of black Schlappen as a beard.

Step 5: Tie in a wing of a rather large bunch of peacock herl, to extend beyond hook.

Step 6: Tie in a collar of orange pig's wool.

Step 7: Complete the head with black thread and cement.

Yerger Note: "A great use of tube flies is to fish spate conditions. They cast and fish much more efficiently than the large, 8/0 or larger single irons used for high water in the past. The

Beauly Snow Fly is an example of an old pattern converted to a tube that has produced very well. The Beauly is a river in Scotland. The 'Snow' part of the pattern name probably refers to the heavy snow melt/run-off conditions under which this fly is used."

A Sami guide holds an Atlantic salmon taken on a tube fly in the Iokanga River in Russia. Bill Hunter photo

Silver-Blue Micro Tube

Tubing: Use the inside liner or sleeve from a Slipstream aluminum tube about 1/2" long. A Size 14 Partridge needle-eye treble fits properly inside the tiny tubing.

Thread: Black.

Step 1: Tie in a sparse wing of 3/4" long blue bucktail evenly distributed around the tube.

Step 2: Tie in two strands of silver tinsel down one side of fly, the same length as bucktail for added flash.

Yerger Note: "Originally tied for summer conditions in Iceland, the Micro Tube has come to be used for low water conditions everywhere. Sometimes they are the only way to move fish."

Skittering Hairy Mary

Tubing: Slipstream plastic tubing, 2" long with the rear ridge cut off. A Partridge needle eye treble in size 10 or 12 fits properly in the tube.

Thread: Black.

Step 1: Drill a small hole into one side of the tube 1/4" behind the front opening.

Step 2: Tie in a tip of oval silver tinsel, leaving enough length to rib the body.

Step 3: Tie in a body of black floss.

Step 4: Rib the body with oval silver tinsel, five turns.

Step 5: Just behind the hole in the side of the tube, tie in a sparse wing of fox squirrel tail distributed evenly, 360° around the tube. The wing should be 1/2" longer than the tube. Tie the wing off and whip finish at this point.

Step 6: Reattach the thread at the front of the tube, ahead of the side hole, and tie in a collar of bright blue around the tube, leaving the side hole uncovered.

Step 7: Whip finish a second time and cement the wraps.

Yerger Note: "This fly, or other patterns tied in this manner, can be fished in a conventional manner, or skittered along the surface, depending upon how you thread the leader through. When the leader is threaded through the side hole instead of the front of the tube fly, it stays on the surface and results in a skittering swing. These skittered tube flies have moved salmon when nothing else would."

Skittering Head

Tubing: 1/2" of 1/8" I.D. plastic tubing, with a short piece of extra soft, 3/16" silicone tubing—available at plastics supply houses—pushed half way up the hard tube. The silicone tubing stretches to fit over a standard tube fly head, holding this modular deer hair head in place.

Thread: Brown.

Step 1: Spin deer hair on one-half the length of the tube and clip it to shape.

Step 2: Whip finish and add head cement.

Yerger Note: "I designed these a few years ago and testing has proven their effectiveness. I tie on a soft tube which can be pushed over the head of a standard (hard plastic) tube to secure it in place. The fly can be fished as is to achieve a regular skittered swing or riffle hitched in the middle of the head to result in an exaggerated skitter."

5

STREAMER TUBE FLIES

A king mackerel fooled by a Sea Bait Ballyhoo. Mark Waslick photo

History

In the mid-1940s, at about the same time tube flies were being developed for Atlantic salmon fishing in the U.K.'s rivers, tube flies began appearing in the Pacific Northwest of the U.S. Unlike the British versions, the first American tube flies were intended for fishing in saltwater, primarily for salmon, and they were trolled just under the surface on floating lines, not cast. Interest in saltwater fishing with flies, hook-tied and on tubes, in the Pacific Northwest coincided with the discovery and promotion of similar opportunities in the Northeast for striped bass, and in Florida for tarpon, bonefish, and permit.

The first commercial tier of tube flies in Washington state, and probably their originator, was Lloyd Peters of Port Angeles. Lloyd's story begins in 1945 when a friend of his younger brother Glen returned from a trip to Campbell River, B.C. with tales of big, hooknosed coho salmon he'd

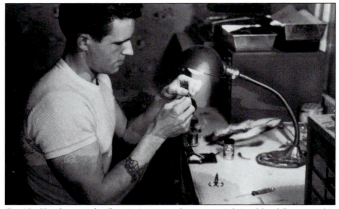

Pacific Northwest tube fly originator and commercial tier Lloyd Peters at his vise in the early 1950s. Photo courtesy of Glen Peters

caught by surface-trolling a five-inch-long, hook-tied, Canadian bucktail streamer behind his boat. He showed the Peters brothers samples of the flies. Lloyd had learned to tie trout flies in junior high school from his hobby class teacher, Mr. Radabaugh. By the time the Canadian bucktails showed up, Lloyd was in his mid-20s and an accomplished tier. He not only copied these crude streamers, but improved their proportions, using his bathtub to test their action. By 1946, he and Glen were trolling with them in the Strait of Juan de Fuca around Port Angeles' Ediz Hook for coho and for Puget Sound resident chinook salmon (known as "blackmouth"). Though they caught lots of fish on these flies, there were problems: the plating on the hooks back then was of very poor quality, so the flies didn't last long in their intended environment; and the silver tinsel-wrapped bodies were quickly shredded by salmon teeth.

Lloyd tried to get around this by tying the flies on a looped strand of 70 pound nylon with the hook pre-snelled at the back end, but wasn't satisfied with the result. He finally solved the problems by tying the flies on short lengths of clear tubing. He began dyeing bucktails to his own specifications and the early tube flies he tied had hair wings of white, topped by green, topped by blue, sometimes topped by black. The wings were tied on one side of the tube only, and he painted eyes on the heads.

By the late 1940s, Lloyd Peter's tube flies were sold up and down the west coast, from Alaska to California, both to commercial and sportfishers. He often named the patterns after the skippers he tied them for ("MacDonald's Special," etc.). His flies were popular with commercial trollers and charter boat captains because they were cheaper and less trouble than bait, which had to be replaced after every fish strike, and they were just as effective. Soon, Lloyd replaced the tinsel bodies with pearl or white fluorescent beads strung up the line between the wing and the hook.

Around the same time, Seattle fly shop owner Roy Patrick and his buddies, Letcher Lambuth and Bill Loherer, were dyeing long hanks of polar bear hair various shades of green, blue, gray, and violet, and layering hairwings to match the coloration of sand lance and herring (see tube conversions of Lambuth's patterns in this chapter), favorites of Pacific chinook and coho salmon. Lambuth's flies were originally tied on hooks and trolled rapidly, a technique known as bucktailing. This was very productive in late summer through fall when coho salmon returned from the Pacific Ocean to enter every river and creek in Puget Sound in huge numbers. Some of the best fishing was in Elliott Bay, in the shadow of the downtown Seattle skyline.

It was also in this period that a handful of adventurous fly fishers—including *Field & Stream's* fishing editor, A. J. McClane—broke away from the trolling paradigm and started casting the big, hook-tied bucktails to coho. McClane used polar bear versions of the popular sand lance and herring patterns to take salmon in British Columbia's Discovery Passage. The Canadian Tourist Board actually produced a short film on coho fishing featuring McClane casting the five-inch-long bucktails with a G3AF floating line. Despite the film and several magazine articles, the concept failed to catch on.

When Lloyd Peters went out of the tying business in the early 1960s, John Gort, also of Port Angeles, began commercially producing tube flies, often using the Lambuth color patterns (Candle Fish, Coronation, Herring). At that time, big coho were still plentiful at Neah Bay from August through October. Gort and Sons manufactured a five-inch, Sliding Coho Fly, the head and wing of which was tied on a short plastic tube, which was trailed by a body of five pearl beads—after Lloyd Peters' basic design. The beads were dipped in acetone to make them iridescent. John sold tube flies to commercial trollers from Alaska to California. His tube flies were also used by sport fishers along the coastlines of California and Florida. In Southern California they were trolled with fly rods for yellowtail.

John Gort's best-selling tube fly for coho was a pearl Mylar-sleeved tube, winged with black over yellow over white bucktail, sometimes tied with a short red beard. For eyes, he would glue on sequins with Testor's glue. The cement caused the sequins to shrink down to fit the contours of the head. He then used single drops of black paint held in a nailset to make the pupils. His tiers all used Herter's vises, and for tube mandrels he cut off the handle shanks from metal files, then chucked them into the vises. The file shanks were very strong steel, and their angled edges and mill marks held the tubes firmly in place.

Before John got out of the business in 1970, he was tying three-inch-long Coronation and Golden Demon tube flies specifically for blackmouth, and sparsely tied five-inch flies for summer chinook salmon. Even though these flies could have been easily cast, they were not. The simple answer as to why is that common wisdom, repeated over and over in books, local newspapers and magazines of the period said to catch salmon in Puget Sound with flies you had to troll big streamers quickly on the surface or drag them behind flashers down deep.

This appears to have been pretty much the case all through the 1960s, and not just in Puget Sound. If cast tube flies were being used in the U.S., it was by individuals whose efforts were not widely publicized. What *was* being widely publicized was saltwater fly fishing in general. Outdoor magazines showed Joe Brooks bringing in 100-pound tarpon, and A. J. McClane based many of his magazine columns on the unparalleled fly fishing in Florida, and explorations of little-known jungle rivers for snook and permit. Perhaps the most dramatic demonstration of saltwater fly fishing of the day was the footage on the "American Sportsman" television program featuring Lee Wulff. Working from a small outboard skiff, armed only with an inexpensive fiberglass rod and large capacity click-drag reel, Wulff hooked and landed a sailfish on a huge, tandem hook streamer of his own design.

Renowned angler/author Lee Wulff designed, tied, and fished this tube sailfish pattern in the 1960s. Fly Fishing in Salt Waters *magazine photo*

By the early 1970s anglers were hitting the beaches, bays, and open ocean along both coasts. They discovered that everything they'd been reading was true: bluefish, striped bass, flounder, rockfish, salmon, tarpon and every other species that roamed the foreshore or pelagic zone of saltwater could be enticed to take a fly. The opening of a two-lane asphalt road from Tiajuana to La Paz unlocked the midriff of the Baja Peninsula to Southern California fly fishers like Harry Kime, who traveled there to tackle Sea of Cortez yellowtail, tuna, dorado, roosterfish, and billfish. New fly patterns were developed by the dozens—some good, some not-so-good—nearly all of which were tied on hooks; but a few American tiers were beginning to experiment with saltwater flies meant for casting that were tied on tubes. Flies like Butorac's Coho Fly and Flasher Fly were shorter in length than standard salmon flies and tied more sparsely; his Baja Trophy Slider was designed to be cast as well as trolled.

In 1976 a hatchery resident coho salmon program was begun by the Washington Department of Fisheries (now the Department of Wildlife) in the protected waters of Puget Sound. This quickly became a productive fly fishery since the coho were voracious feeders and of a size that could be handled nicely on a mid-weight trout rod. From January through May these frisky and ever-hungry salmon would smack just about any pattern that looked like a cocapod or shrimp. By early June, the coho were approaching three pounds in weight and because they needed more to sustain them, switched their primary food source to sand lance and small herring. This brought about a flurry of fly tying by the fledgling cadre of Washington saltwater salmon anglers, resulting in dozens of new baitfish dressings.

In the spring of 1977 Garry Sandstrom, a young biology graduate from Tacoma, Washington, also caught up in the Puget Sound coho fishery felt that what was needed was a fly with a long silhouette to better imitate a baitfish. Such a fly would also have the hook at the very end of the tube, better to hook cohos which are notorious short-strikers. After a bit of research, Sandstrom came up with his version of a baitfish tied on a four-inch section of plastic pressure gauge tubing. These early tube flies, simple blue and white bucktails on a tube sleeved with silver Mylar piping, were an immediate hit with coho, chinook—and local anglers.

New tube fly patterns soon burst upon the Puget Sound angling scene tied by Dave Wands, Brian Steel, Bruce Ferguson, and other local saltwater fly fishers. The use of cast tube flies in Pacific Northwest waters was first documented in 1985 in *Fly Fishing for Pacific Salmon*. At the time, the popularity of tube flies for salmon seemed to be localized to the saltwater anglers of Washington, but in fact, a tube renaissance was well underway in far-flung corners of the angling world, with most of the innovation concentrated on developing more productive and realistic saltwater patterns.

In Europe, fly tiers had begun to dress tubes with baitfish patterns intended for sea trout in the estuaries of Norway, Finland, Sweden, and the British Isles. These dressings were a departure from traditional Atlantic salmon tube flies of British influence,

A pair of Tidemark commercially-tied tube flies from the mid-1980s and an early Garry Sandstrom Baja tube fly of the same period.

being realistic rather than fanciful, long and slim, more in keeping with the bait salmon and sea trout key on while in their saltwater feeding habit. The deadly effectiveness of these sparse, slender tube dressings was soon proven on Atlantic salmon and sea trout in Scandinavian waters, on large Argentine brown trout and B.C.'s Dean River steelhead, and on Baja dorado and billfish.

At the current stage of tube streamer development, the trend toward realism in appearance and fly action is very evident, with much of the impetus coming from improved materials and tying techniques. This movement is also being driven by a spreading awareness among fly fishers that realistic tube flies work well on a wide variety of species.

TUBE CONVERSIONS OF TRADITIONAL STREAMERS

This section explains how conventional, hook-tied streamer patterns can be adapted to tubes. These tying instructions demonstrate some ways that proven flies can be modified to fit a tube, but not the *only* ways.

A hooked dorado goes airborne. Les Johnson photo

Steve Abel (Camarillo, California)
Abel Anchovy
Tied by Les Johnson

Tubing: 3/4" of 1/8" O.D. hard plastic tubing, with a 1" long, 3/16" vinyl hook holder.
Thread: Black or chartreuse, Size A.

Step 1: Insert the hard tubing into the soft tubing about 1/2" and put it on your vise, soft tube first. On top of the soft tube, just back from the front edge of the join, tie on a fairly thick, tapered bunch of 2 1/2" white bucktail, FisHair or Polar Hair. Whatever the material, use the same type throughout the fly.

Step 2: Tie in about a dozen 1 1/4" strands of red Flashabou, Crystal Hair or Krystal Flash on top of the white material as a beard. Rotate the tube 180° on your vise, so this part becomes the belly of the fly.

Step 3: Tie in a fairly thick, tapered bunch of 3 1/2" white hair of the same type as in **Step 1**.

Step 4: On top of that, tie in a matching tapered bunch of green hair. Top that with about half as much blue hair, slightly shorter in length, and also tapered.

Step 5: Tie in 15 to 20 strands of silver Flashabou. Add another 15 to 20 strands of pearl Flashabou on top of the silver.

Step 6: On top of that, tie in 10 to 15 strands of peacock herl. This topping should be the same length as the green and white wing.

Step 7: Whip finish the head, and glue in place with Zap-A-Gap large doll eyes (white with black pupil), the bigger the better. The sample fly uses 12mm eyes. Finish the head with a hot glue gun, or epoxy.

Abel Note: "I began designing the Abel Anchovy about 1985 for shark fishing and at first it was pretty universally ignored. Sharks definitely preferred the real thing—frozen, chummed anchovies. One day I noticed that the chummed anchovies loosed a spray of scales when they hit the water, forming sort of a halo effect. I decided to imitate these loose scales by using strands of silver and pearl Flashabou, then added over-size eyes as well. Results were immediate. This fly has taken blue and mako sharks, peacock bass, dorado, chinook salmon, Pacific bonito, skipjack, barracuda, yellowtail, tarpon, and sailfish."

Dan Blanton (San Jose, California)
Sar-Mul-Mac

Tubing: 1" of 1/8" hard plastic tubing with 1" of 3/16" vinyl tubing over the rear for a 1/2" hook holder. For a fast-sinking Sar-Mul-Mac, substitute a 1" to 1 1/2" length of brass tubing in place of the hard plastic.
Thread: Danville's flat waxed nylon in white.

Step 1: Tie a medium-sized bunch of bucktail, the length of which will determine overall length of the fly, onto the section where the two pieces of connected tubing overlap.

Step 2: On either side of the bucktail, tie in six white saddle hackles as long as the bucktail.

Step 3: Along the saddle hackles, on both sides, attach several strands of multi-colored Krystal Flash and five strands of silver Flashabou.

Step 4: Rotate the tube 180° on your vise and tie in medium bunch of white bucktail the same length as the first.

Step 5: Rotate the tube 180° on your vise again and tie in two matching green dyed grizzly saddle hackles approximately the same length as the white saddle hackles, tent style over the white hackles.

Step 6: Top with a sparse bunch of aqua or blue Krystal Flash, over which is added several strands of peacock herl with the butts left long to extend beyond the front end of the tube. Secure with thread, but do not trim butt ends of the herl.

Step 7: Tie in teal flank feather cheeks on either side (optional).

Step 8: Add two turns of red chenille ahead of the wing as gills. Be sure that the chenille is wrapped under the peacock herl.

Step 9: Ahead of the red chenille, tie in white chenille and wrap it forward to the end of the tube. Be sure that white chenille is also wrapped under the peacock herl.

Step 10: Pull the peacock herl butts over the chenille and tie them off at the nose. Trim the excess. Whip finish the thread, and give the wraps a touch of Dave's Flexament.

Step 11: Cement a pair of large doll's eyes (if you use the post-style eyes, trim off the posts) to the head with Goop or thinned Aqua Seal.

Blanton Note: "I don't usually use tube flies since I prefer the action I can get with a fly tied on a hook. My Sar-Mul-Mac has been popular as a Baja pattern for more than 20 years. It has been used primarily as a trolling fly, since most fly rodders couldn't cast the ones that were 10 to 12 inches long. It is a great fish-finder for billfish and dorado."

Johnson Note: "When debarking from our panga after a brisk day of fishing for dorado, skippies and bonito north of Isla Coronado, out of Loreto, Mexico, Mark Mandell and I met two Southern California anglers who had also enjoyed a lot of hookups. As it turned out we were all using tube flies. The only pattern the two anglers carried were several sizes and variations of the Dan Blanton Sar-Mul-Mac, including one with a lot of red in it that had been their killer of the day."

Dan Blanton and Bob Edgely
Sea Arrow Squid
Tied by Mark Mandell

Tubing: 2" of 1/8" hard white plastic tubing and 1 1/2" of 3/16" vinyl tubing.
Thread: White Monocord.

Step 1: Insert 2" of white plastic tubing into 1 1/2" vinyl tubing 3/8". Find the curve of the vinyl tubing and mark the end of the white tubing to indicate the top side. Put the tube on your vise, and overwrap join area with thread. Wrap thread back to 1/2" from the rear end of the tube. Select a dozen 3" white saddle hackles. Leaving the marabou fluff on the hackle butts, tie the saddles in all around the tube. The saddles should point in all directions. Trim off the excess, tie down the butts and cement.

Step 2: Turn the tube so its side is facing up. On top of the tube, tie in a sparse 3" bunch of pearl Krystal Flash. Rotate the tube 180° and on top of the tube tie in a matching bunch of pearl Krystal Flash. Select a pair of 4 1/2" white saddle hackles. Leaving the fluff on the butts, tips flaring out, tie one of these on top of each of the bunches of pearl Krystal Flash. Wrap the butts down, trim excess and cement. Tie in eight to ten 4 1/2" strands of lavender Krystal Flash on either side of the tube. The bunches of lavender Krystal Flash should run down the center of each of the long white saddles.

Step 3: With sidecutters, trim the plastic posts off a pair of amber and black 10mm plastic doll's eyes. Trim the posts flush with the back of the eyes. Then, using a hand drill and a 5/64" bit, bore a back to front hole through the center of the eyes. Cut a 2" piece of 80 pound monofilament and using a match, melt the tip of one end into a small blob; color the blob with a black marker. Insert the unmelted end of the mono into the hole in the front of the eye and pull the blob

down into the hole. Trim the excess protruding blob with scissors. Bend the mono so it makes a right angle as soon as it exits the back of the eye. Flatten the exiting portion of mono with pliers. Tie these prepared doll's eyes on the sides of the tube. The centers of the eyes should be about 1/2" from the back end of the tube and surrounded by marabou fluff. Wrap the mono butts down with thread, trim excess and cement well.

Step 4: Tie in a long piece of white polypro yarn on the white plastic tube, 1" in front of the start of the soft tubing. Wrap the yarn to the eyes and back, creating an even taper 1 1/2" long. Trim the excess yarn, and overwrap with thread back to the eyes.

Step 5: On top of the tube, between the eyes, tie in some large white chenille. In tight turns, wrap the chenille forward on the tube 1 1/4". Then turn the tube so the side is facing up. Cut a 2" piece of white polypro yarn, tie it to the top of the tube with two tight turns of thread at the yarn's midpoint. Rotate the tube 180°. Repeat with another 2" piece of white polypro. Return the tube to the top up position. Push the thread wraps tight with your fingernail, and then advance the chenille forward one snug turn. Repeat this procedure five or six more times, until you are 1/2" from front end of tube. At this point, wrap the chenille forward another 1/4", tie it down and trim the excess. Whip finish and cement.

Step 6: Tease or comb out the polypro fibers into an even mat on both sides of the tube. They should be butterfly wing shaped. Soak the fibers well with Dave's Flexament. Let dry thoroughly. With scissors, trim the polypro into an arrow shape. Apply a second coat of Flexament. Before the cement is completely dry, pinch down the edges of the arrow.

Mandell Note: This standard fly is a fairly complicated and time-consuming pattern to tie; it has lots of fragile saddle hackles hanging off the rear end; and it is intended to be fished in saltwater where who-knows-what is going to chomp on it. These three factors, in my opinion, make it a prime candidate for conversion to a tube."

Whistler
Tied by Mark Mandell

Tubing: Various lengths of hard plastic, and brass, copper, and aluminum tubing.
Thread: Fluorescent red 6/0.

Step 1: Put a 1" lined brass tube on your vise and attach tying thread. Tie in a piece of medium flat silver Mylar 1/4" from the front end of the tube. Wrap the Mylar to the rear end of the tube in tight, close turns, then wrap it back to the head. Tie down the Mylar, trim the excess and whip finish. Apply Joli Glaze, Flexament or 5-minute epoxy to Mylar and wraps. Let dry.

Step 2: Rotate the tube 180° in the vise. On top of the tube, 1/4" from the front end, tie in a bunch of 2 1/2" long white bucktail or FisHair. Rotate the tube 180° again. Tie in a matching bunch of white bucktail or FisHair.

Step 3: Select six white saddle hackles 4" long. Tie three of the hackles to the side of the tube, with the feathers' curve pointing in. Tie the other three to the other side of the tube. Top these hackles on both sides with one grizzly saddle, of the same length. Along the back of the fly add a small bunch of silver Flashabou, 4" long. On top of the Flashabou, tie in a small bunch of peacock herl, 4" long.

Step 4: Select a fluorescent red marabou blood feather with fibers about 1 1/2" long. Tie it in at the shoulder of the wing, then wrap it around the tube several times. Tie off the marabou and trim away the excess.

Step 5: Take a pair of large silver bead chain eyes and tie them on top of the tube, just ahead of the wing. Figure-eight the eyes with thread, securing them well, then build up a neatly tapered head with thread. Whip finish and Joli Glaze or 5-minute epoxy the head.

Mandell Note: This Dan Blanton saltwater standard is also tied in orange and black, and orange and yellow."

Steve Shelley releases a four-pound pink salmon at Queen Charlotte Islands, British Columbia. Les Johnson photo

Errol Champion (Juneau, Alaska)
Salmon Treat
Tied by Mark Mandell

Tubing: 1 1/2" of 1/8" hard plastic tubing.
Thread: Clear monofilament.

Step 1: Put 1 1/2" of 1/8" plastic tubing on your tube vise, natural curve pointing down. Slip 2" of medium silver Mylar piping over the front of the tube, extending it about 1" past the tube's rear end. Tie it down at the rear of the tube with mono thread and whip finish. Tie it down at the head with mono thread, whip finish, and Joli Glaze or 5-minute epoxy body and wraps.

Step 2: As a throat, tie in together a red and white saddle hackle 1/2" from the front end of the tube. After wrapping several turns of hackle, tie it off with thread and secure it. Trim all the hackle from the top of the tube, where the wing will go.

Step 3: Tie in a sparse 3 1/2" wing of polar bear or white FisHair, then a slightly longer but equally sparse bunch of green FisHair, topped by slightly longer purple FisHair. (This fly is also tied with a white, yellow, and lime green wing, or a white, yellow, and hot orange wing.) Trim excess and cement.

Step 4: Take the cotton core out of 1 1/2" or so of medium silver piping, draw a line of Super Glue down the length of it, then let it dry completely. Cut the piping along the glue line. Fit the sheet of silver Mylar you've created to the underside of the head and wrap it down with a few turns of mono thread. Trim excess Mylar at the nose and apply the rest of the sheet to the top of the head. Bind the Mylar sheets down with thread so they conform to the shape of the head. Trim excess Mylar from around the back of the head.

Step 5: Lay about ten strands of 4" peacock herl on top of last layer of FisHair, letting it extend over the nose of fly. Compress the herl so it makes a stripe down the center of the head, and tie it down with mono thread. Stick on silver 5/32" Witchcraft eyes, put two turns of mono thread over each eye, and whip finish. Joli Glaze or epoxy the head.

Mandell Note: "This is a tube version of Champion's pattern, which was designed for southeastern Alaska waters. If you can find Mylar piping in the color and size you need, obviously you don't have to go to the trouble of making a *sheet* and then binding it down—just slide on the correctly-sized piping and wrap it down with mono. At one point in tying the flies for this book, Les and I were stuck with piping that was too small for the heads we wanted to make. This is one way we got around it. Another way is to flatten the piping against the head with wraps of mono thread *without* making a sheet out of it. This, of course, uses up more piping and it creates a slightly bulkier head."

Dr. Lloyd Day (Quesnel, British Columbia)
Carey Special
Tied by Joe Butorac

Tubing: 1/2 to 2" of 1/8" hard plastic tubing.
Thread: Black.

Step 1: At the rear of the tube, tie in a piece of flat, fine silver tinsel or pearl Mylar for the ribbing. If desired, add wraps of lead fuse wire for a weighted fly.

Step 2: Build a body of black (or brown or green) wool or dubbing. Tie down the wool with thread and trim the excess.

Step 3: Rib forward five turns with the tinsel or Mylar.

Step 4: Tie in a pheasant rump hackle, wet fly style. The hackle tips should extend past the end of the tube about 1/3 of its length. Wrap three turns of hackle, tie it down with thread, and trim the excess.

Step 5: Build a neat head with black thread, whip finish, and cement.

Butorac Note: "Depending on the length of the fly, I normally fish a size 8 to a size 1, up-eyed, short shanked bait hook with this pattern. This pattern was first used in the 1930s for Kamloops trout in British Columbia. It is intended to simulate a dragonfly nymph."

Don Gapen (Nipigon, Ontario, Canada)
Marabou Muddler
Tied by Garry Sandstrom

Tubing: 1 3/4" to 3" of 1/8" hard plastic tubing, depending on the size of the fly.
Thread: Black.

Step 1: Slide a piece of small gold Mylar piping over the plastic tube. Secure the piping with thread at both ends, tying it off flush with the front of the tube and leaving it a bit longer than the tube in back. After you've tied the piping down, unravel it at the rear to form a tail 1/4" long. Attach two strands of gold Krystal Flash along either side of the tube. Be sure to leave enough room for the spun deer hair head at the front of the tube.

Step 2: Attach a small clump of red fox squirrel tail about 3/8" from the front end of the tube. The tips should extend to the frayed ends of the gold Mylar.

Step 3: Select two brown grizzly marabou feathers. Tie them flat on top of the squirrel tail.

Step 4: Where the marabou is attached, tie in two small clumps of red Krystal Flash approximately 3/8" long, to act as gills.

Step 5: For pectoral fins, tie in one grouse or hen back feather over the red Krystal Flash on either side of the tube.

Step 6: Attach a pair of 6/32" painted, non-lead eyes to the front of the tube.

Step 7: Form a dubbing loop at the pectoral fin junction, insert some brown deer hair and spin it tightly.

Step 8: Wrap the spun hair forward toward the eyes, between the eyes and finish at the front end of tube.

Step 9: Shape head to sculpin profile and whip finish.

Sandstrom Note: "I began using this fly because I wanted a more durable Muddler, one that hooked and held fish more efficiently. Short shank hooks that work well with tube flies are less prone to working out and by being able to use a smaller hook on a large fly, it seems to inflict less damage on the fish. This fly has taken browns, rainbows and sea-run cutthroat."

Harold Gibbs (Barrington, Rhode Island)
Gibbs' Striper Bucktail
Tied by Mark Mandell

Tubing: 1 3/8" of 1/8" hard plastic tubing. The tube and wing length should match the bait size. See Note below.
Thread: Black.

Step 1: Put the plastic tube on your vise and attach the tying thread. Tie in a piece of flat silver tinsel at the rear of the tube, advance the thread to the front of the tube. Wrap the tinsel forward to the head. Tie down tinsel at the front, trim excess tinsel, and cover the thread wraps and tinsel with Flexament or Joli Glaze. Let dry.

Step 2: Match a pair of guinea hen breast feathers and coat them on both sides with Flexament. Let them dry. Tie in a sparse bunch of red hackle fibers at the throat. For the wing, tie in a sparse bunch of 3 1/4" white or polar bear FisHair (see Note below), then an even sparser bunch of medium blue FisHair, topped by white or polar bear FisHair the same volume as the first.

Step 3: Position the guinea feathers on either side of the body and tie them in at the head. Build up the head with black thread and whip finish. Lacquer or epoxy the wraps.

Mandell Note: "In his book, *Streamer Fly Tying and Fishing* (Stackpole Books, 1970), Joseph Bates quotes the fly's originator, Harold Gibbs, as saying he liked to tie it on short shank 1/0 to 3/0 hooks. Gibbs also said he made his wings rather short, about twice the length of the hook shank, this to match the size of the baitfish."

Ned Grey (Montrose, California)
Matuka Streaker
Tied by Garry Sandstrom

Tubing: 5" of 1/8" hard plastic tubing.
Thread: White Monocord.

Step 1: Slide a piece of small pearl Mylar piping over the plastic tube. Secure the piping with thread at both ends, tying it off flush with the front of the tube and leaving it a bit longer than the tube in back. After you've tied the piping down, unravel it at the rear to form a tail.

Step 2: Tie in a pair of matched peacock swords at the front of the tube. Whip finish.

Step 3: Lift the swords out of the way and coat the top of the tube with 5-minute epoxy. Rotate the tube 180°, holding the peacock against the tube to allow the epoxy to run into the peacock sword. Let dry.

Step 4: Tie in a sparse bunch of white polar bear, bucktail, or FisHair, the length of the body for the fly's belly.

Step 5: Tie in a few strands of red Krystal Flash at the throat.

Step 6: Tie in a short bunch of yellow polar bear, bucktail, or FisHair for cheeks on each side. Rotate the fly so the peacock sword is once again on top.

Step 7: On each side of the peacock sword, tie in a short

bunch of peacock Krystal Flash topped with a few strands of pearl Flashabou.

Step 8: Complete the head with close turns of micro tinsel to match the color of the peacock sword. Whip finish. Epoxy large (5mm) doll's eyes (white background, black pupil) to the sides of the head. Apply a light coat of epoxy to the thread wraps and around the eyes.

Sandstrom Note: "I've always liked the Streaker except for the common problem of the peacock breaking after taking just a few fish. By tying the pattern on a tube and using epoxy to bond the stem of the peacock sword onto the tube I now have a nearly indestructible Streaker."

Humboldt Bay Anchovy
(originator unknown)
Tied by Mark Mandell

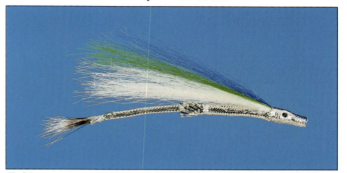

Tubing: 1 3/4" of 1/8" hard plastic tubing, keyholed to take a hook eye (see "Materials, Tools, Rigging" chapter).
Thread: Clear monofilament thread and white Monocord.

Step 1: Use a rubber leader straightener to take most of the curve out of a long section of 40 to 60-pound hard monofilament leader material, then cut off a 3" piece. Put one end of the hard mono in the jaws of a standard tying vise with natural curve of the mono pointing down. With white Monocord thread, tie equal bunches of gray squirrel tail to the top and bottom sides of the free end of leader material. Zap-A-Gap or 5-minute epoxy the wraps. When they're dry, cut off the excess leader material between the squirrel tail, so it looks like a single bunch of widely flared hair. Remove the leader piece from the vise and slide 1 3/4" of small silver Mylar piping over front end of the leader material. Move the piping down until it covers the wraps on the squirrel tail. Put the leader material back in the vise, front end first, and bind the piping down with clear mono thread at the tail and whip finish. Then tie down the Mylar at the front and whip finish. Trim the excess Mylar at the tail, Joli Glaze or Flexament the wrappings and the Mylar.

Step 2: Flatten the first 1 1/2" of the front end of the leader material between the jaws of the pliers. Then put 1 3/4" of 1/8" hard plastic tubing onto your tube vise, the non-keyholed end first. With white Monocord thread tie the leader part of the tail section on top of the tube, making sure that the natural curves of both the tube and the tail sections line up. Trim the front end of the leader material back so at least 5/8" of the plastic tube remains uncovered—this is for the tapered nose of the fly. Whip finish, then Zap-A-Gap or epoxy the wraps.

Step 3: Reverse the tube in your vise. Slide some medium silver piping over the plastic tube. It should be long enough to cover the join of the tail section. Tie it down at the tail end with mono thread, then fray out the Mylar, leaving a 3/8" silver skirt over the join area. Whip finish. Tie the Mylar piping down at the head, whip finish, and coat whole thing with Joli Glaze or Dave's Flexament. Let dry.

Step 4: Tie in a sparse 3" wing of polar bear FisHair topped by an equal amount of green FisHair. The tips of the wing should be shorter than the squirrel tail, as shown. Build up the rear of the head with mono thread and make it taper down at the nose.

Step 5: Take the cotton core out of 1 1/2" or so of medium silver piping, draw a line of Super Glue down the length of it, then let it dry completely. Cut the piping along the glue line. Fit the sheet of silver Mylar you've created to the underside of the head and wrap it against the tube with a few turns of mono thread. Trim the excess Mylar at the nose and apply the rest of the sheet to the top of the head. Bind the Mylar sheets down with thread so they conform to the shape of the head. Trim the excess Mylar from around the back of the head.

Step 6: Put on a top wing of medium blue FisHair, adjust it so it extends past the end of the nose in front, and is as long in back as the underwing, then tie it down with a few turns of thread. Apply 7/32" silver Witchcraft eyes, putting two turns of mono thread over each eye, and then wrap whole head with mono thread, adjusting the blue FisHair to make a neat dorsal stripe to the tip of the tube. Whip finish. Trim excess Mylar and FisHair from the nose. Apply several coats of Joli Glaze, a day apart, to head and body. Or one thin coat of 5-minute epoxy.

David Hurn (Victoria, British Columbia)
Hurn's Candlefish
Tied by Les Johnson

Tubing: 1 1/4" plastic Slipstream tube.
Thread: Clear monofilament.

Step 1: Cut a 2" piece of small silver Mylar piping and remove the core. Slide the piping over the hard tube and tie it down about 1/8" from the front end of the tube. Fray out the Mylar up to the back end of the tube.

Step 2: On top of the tube, tie in a 2 3/4" bunch of white polar bear hair.

Step 3: On top of that, tie in a sparse bunch of red polar bear, same length.

Step 4: Top that with a very sparse bunch of white polar bear, followed by a sparse bunch of pale green polar bear.

Step 5: Top the wing with a half dozen strands of peacock herl, the same length as the wing. With the mono thread, wrap down the butts of the wing material to make a neat dorsal stripe on the head. Trim the excess material from the nose of the fly.

Step 6: Stick on Witchcraft eyes and wrap them with a turn of monofilament thread.

Step 7: Whip finish and give the head a light coat of epoxy.

Hal Janssen (Santa Rosa, California)
Janssen Striper Fly
Tied by Les Johnson

Tubing: 1" to 2" Slipstream plastic tube for small flies. For larger flies, use 1 1/2" of 1/8" hard plastic tubing with 1 1/2" of 3/16" vinyl tubing as hook holder.
Thread: Clear monofilament.

Step 1: Cut a piece of pearl Mylar piping that is three times the length of the tube you're going to use. (For a 3/4" inch tube, use 2 1/4" of piping.) Slide the piping over the end of the tube and put it on your vise. With mono thread, tie the piping down about 1/8" from the front end of the tube. Wrap the thread back 1/4" toward the rear of the tube, binding down the piping. Fray out the Mylar up to the back end of the tube.

Step 2: On top of the tube, tie in a very sparse bunch of white bucktail, slightly longer than the Mylar. This is the belly of the fly.

Step 3: Rotate the fly 180° on your vise.

Step 4: On top of the tube, tie in a very sparse bunch of white bucktail, the same length as the belly.

Step 5: Tie in a very sparse bunch of blue bucktail over the white, same length.

Step 6: Tie in a sparse bunch of bright green bucktail over the blue, same length.

Step 7: Complete the head by wrapping down the butts of the green bucktail with mono thread to form a neat dorsal stripe. Trim the excess bucktail. Whip finish the head. Stick on silver Witchcraft eyes and epoxy the head.

Johnson Note: "Janssen developed the Striper Fly in 1958 to imitate the grunion, a favorite forage fish of striped bass in the San Francisco Bay area. The Striper Fly quickly became popular not only for stripers but for salmon, and remains one of the top patterns for fishing kelp bass and rock fish in the waters along the north Marin coast."

Bernard "Lefty" Kreh (Hunt Valley, Maryland)
Lefty's Deceiver
Tied by Les Johnson

Tubing: 1 1/2" of 1/8" hard plastic tubing with 1" of 3/16" vinyl tubing as a hook holder.

Thread: White floss for all tying steps except the finishing of the head, where clear monofilament is used.

Step 1: Select eight matching hackles, four from each side of a good grade saddle patch to suit the overall length of the fly. Align the matching hackles, four on each side so that the concave sides face each other. You do not want the hackles to splay out. Tie the hackles in, one set on each side of the tube, lashing them to the section where the two joined pieces of tubing overlap. Tie off and trim the floss.

Step 2: Cut a short length of small silver Mylar piping and slip it over the tube, expanding it slightly so it fits over the butts of the saddle hackles. Reattach the floss and tie the Mylar off at the front of the tube.

Step 3: Build up the front, shoulder section of the fly with small bunches of white bucktail all the way around the tube. Leave a slight gap at the bottom to accommodate the hook eye. Bucktail should extend well beyond the end of the tube to be about 1/3 the length of the fly.

Step 4: Top this with a sparse bunch of contrasting dyed bucktail to match the type of baitfish you are imitating. Over the contrasting bucktail, tie in several strands of peacock herl, Krystal Flash or Flashabou to complete the fly.

Step 5: Cut and trim the white floss. Attach the clear monofilament tying thread.

Step 6: Add a few strands of pearl or silver Flashabou on each side and contrasting Flashabou on top of the fly (optional).

Step 7: Rotate the tube 180° on your vise. Tie in several strands of red Flashabou for a throat.

Step 8: Lightly coat the head with Dave's Flexament.

Step 9: Stick on Witchcraft eyes to match the size of the fly.

Step 10: Complete the head with a light coat of epoxy.

Johnson Note: "Lefty's Deceiver is one of the best patterns ever to grace a fly box, or a game fish's jaw. With the Deceiver, Lefty Kreh has given us a good basic baitfish design that can be fine-tuned by the use of various colors and types of feathers, bucktail, and glittery synthetics to imitate just about any creature that swims. There are examples of several variations of Lefty's Deceiver in the color plates, but what can be done with this highly versatile pattern is really only limited by the tier's imagination. In terms of sheer productivity on a wide range of species, it is a hard act to match. I have personally fished it from Alaska to Mexico, taking small, feeder cohos, mature coho and chinook, and bull dorado. The pattern has been widely imitated and is the basis for many commercial spin-offs, often without proper credit. Whatever name a variation on the Lefty's Deceiver theme may be given by an individual tier though, it can always be recognized by its distinctive outline—the long, wispy hackle tail and bucktail front to build a bulky baitfish shape."

Letcher Lambuth (Seattle, Washington)

The great saltwater bucktail dressings of the Pacific Northwest, pioneered by the late Letcher Lambuth in the 1940s and refined with kibitzing from his friends, Bill Loherer of Loherer's Sporting Goods, Roy Patrick, owner of Patrick's Fly Shop, and Zell Parkhurst, were dressed strictly on hooks and used primarily for trolling with a fly rod. The contribution Lambuth, Loherer, Patrick, and Parkhurst made to saltwater fly fishing in Washington's Puget Sound, the Strait of Juan de Fuca, and Campbell River is legendary among anglers in Washington and British Columbia, but not widely recognized elsewhere in the American angling community. Fortunately, Joseph Bates carefully chronicled their work in *Streamer Fly Tying and Fishing*. Many of the patterns Lambuth produced in collaboration with his friends became steady fish producers and remain popular today. While these fine gentlemen have departed our ranks, they leave behind a legacy of outstanding saltwater fly tying development, a cornerstone upon which contemporary fly tiers are still building.

Les Johnson took this chunky coho on a Lambuth Candle Fish tube fly at first light in the sea lanes of the straight of San Juan de Fuca off Sekiu, Washington in September 1992. Mark Mandell photo

Lambuth Candle Fish
Tied by Les Johnson

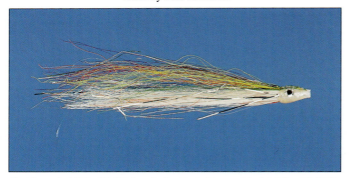

Tubing: 1 1/2" of 1/8" hard plastic tubing with 1 1/2" of 3/16" vinyl tubing for a hook holder. For the smallest imitations, 1 1/2" to 3" in overall length, use plastic Slipstream tubes 1/2" to 1" long, reducing the material to maintain a well-proportioned dressing.

Thread: Clear monofilament.

Step 1: Start the thread on the soft tubing, a bit back from its front edge. Tie in a few strands of pink or red bucktail, FisHair, or Super Hair to mark the top of the tube.

Step 2: Develop a baitfish body shape with a sparse, even layer of white FisHair all the way around the tube, leaving a slight gap at the bottom to accommodate the hook.

Step 3: Over the FisHair, on each side of the tube, add a few strands of silver and pearl Flashabou.

Step 4: Tie in an additional sparse bunch of white FisHair on top of the tube.

Step 5: Build the first section of the three-part FisHair wing by tying in a very sparse bunch of pale green under dark blue FisHair.

Step 6: Tie in a very sparse bunch of red FisHair as a midwing.

Step 7: Complete the wing with a very sparse bunch of green under violet FisHair.

Step 8: Top the wing with a few strands of blue and green Flashabou extending to end of the FisHair. With the mono thread, wrap the butts of the wing material down over the head, making a neat dorsal stripe. Trim the excess material from the front of the tube.

Step 9: Rotate the tube 180° on your vise and add a few strands of red or fluorescent orange Flashabou as a throat. Clip short.

Step 10: Stick on Witchcraft eyes, then secure them in place with a turn or two of thread.

Step 11: Finish the head with a light coat of epoxy.

Johnson Note: "A range of fly sizes from three to five inches long will cover most situations where the Candle Fish pattern is required. Sand lance, which the Candle Fish pattern imitates, are found along the west coast in lengths from one-and-one-half to six inches, with sizes overlapping at times depending on emergences. Most of the original patterns designed by Lambuth and his pals were dressed with bucktail but more often, polar bear, which accepts dyes very well to produce vivid colors. Wherever it remains a legal tying material, polar bear is still very popular due to its sheen, durability and action in the water. Most tiers will find, however that substituting either bucktail, African goat, or any of the synthetic hair materials will make up into a fine, fish-taking fly."

Lambuth Herring
Tied by Les Johnson

Tubing: 1 1/2" of 1/8" hard plastic tubing with 1 1/2" of 3/16" vinyl tubing as a hook holder. For a fast-sinking pattern, substitute a 1 1/2" copper tube for the hard plastic. Overall fly length is four to seven inches (adult herring range from six to twelve inches in length).

Thread: Clear monofilament.

Step 1: Start the thread on the soft tubing, a bit back from its front edge. Tie in a few strands of pink or red bucktail, FisHair, or Super Hair to mark the top of the tube.

Step 2: Develop a baitfish body shape with a sparse, even layer of white FisHair all the way around the tube, leaving a slight gap at the bottom to accommodate the hook.

Step 3: Add a few strands of pearl and silver Krystal Flash on either side, the same length as the FisHair.

Step 4: Tie in an additional sparse, tapered bunch of white FisHair, same length, on top of the tube.

Step 5: Build the first layer of a three-part, tapered wing using equal amounts of pale green and mouse gray FisHair, mixed, and slightly longer than the white.

Step 6: Tie in a sparse bunch of tapered dark green FisHair as a midwing.

Step 7: Complete the wing using sparse, tapered and equal amounts of dark green under dark blue FisHair.

Step 8: Top with a few strands of black Krystal Flash, extending the full length of the wing. With the mono thread, wrap the butts of the wing material down over the head, making a neat dorsal stripe. Trim the excess material from the front of the tube.

Step 9: Rotate the tube 180° on the vise and tie in a few strands of red or fluorescent orange Flashabou as a throat. Clip short.

Step 10: Stick on Witchcraft eyes, then secure them in place with a few turns of clear monofilament.

Step 11: Whip finish and cover the head with a thin coat of epoxy.

Johnson Note: "The Lambuth Herring pattern was popular with anglers fishing coho salmon out of Neah Bay and Sekiu on the northwest tip of Washington's Strait of Juan de Fuca. While the Herring did indeed bring slashing strikes from big, broad-shouldered adult coho salmon, it was also effective for chinook holding along the kelp beds closer to shore."

Coronation
Tied by Les Johnson

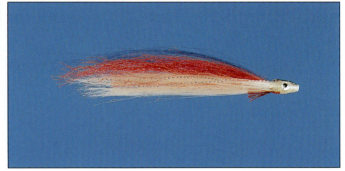

This is an attractor pattern rather than a specific imitation. It works well in a range of sizes from four to seven inches in length.

Tubing: 1 1/2" of 1/8" hard plastic tubing with 1 1/2" of 3/16" vinyl for a hook holder.
Thread: Clear monofilament.

Step 1: Start the thread on the soft tubing, a bit back from its front edge. Tie in a few strands of pink or red bucktail, FisHair, or Super Hair to mark the top of the tube.

Step 2: Develop a baitfish body shape with a medium-sized layer of white FisHair all the way around the tube, leaving a slight gap at the bottom to accommodate the hook.

Step 3: Tie in an additional sparse bunch of white FisHair on top of the tube.

Step 4: Build the first layer of a three-part wing with a medium sized bunch of white FisHair.

Step 5: Tie a medium bunch of red FisHair over the white.

Step 6: Tie a medium bunch of dark blue FisHair over the red. With the mono thread, wrap the butts of the wing material down over the head, making a neat blue dorsal stripe.

Step 7: Add a few strands of silver Flashabou or Krystal Flash at the base of the wing on each side. They should be as long as the wing and extend past the nose of the fly in front. Tie these strands down with mono thread to make a line of silver below and touching the blue dorsal stripe, the full length of the fly head. Trim the excess material from the front of the tube.

Step 8: Rotate the tube 180° on your vise and tie in a sparse bunch of red or fluorescent orange Flashabou as a throat. Clip short.

Step 9: Stick on Witchcraft eyes, and secure them in place with a few turns of clear monofilament.

Step 10: Finish the head with light coat of epoxy.

Johnson Note: The Coronation was destined to be the most inspirational of Lambuth's coho patterns, probably because it was simpler and quicker to tie than either the Candle Fish or Herring. From the 1940s through 1960s, during the heyday of Puget Sound salmon runs when the kings were showing at the Mid-Channel Bank and Shilshole Bay, or coho, then known as the 'silver hordes', were marshalling off Double Bluff or Point Defiance, cranking out a few flies fast was the order of the day.

"The color variations that followed the Coronation, as originally listed in *Streamer Fly Tying and Fishing*, were: Green over white, blue over white, brown over white, green over yellow over white, blue over green over white, green over red over white, gray over medium green over fuchsia over white, blue over green over yellow over white and gray over green over peach over white. All of these color combinations are established salmon-takers in saltwater."

Homer Rhode, Jr. (Miami, Florida)
Homer Rhode's Tarpon Steamer
Tied by Les Johnson

Tubing: 1" Slipstream plastic, aluminum, or brass with 1 1/2" of 3/16" vinyl tubing over the back as a hook holder. The plastic center sleeve of the tube can be pushed out to accommodate a heavy monofilament or wire shock tippet.
Thread: Strong nylon or waxed floss in hot orange.

Step 1: Insert the hard tubing into the soft hook holder 1/2" and put it on your vise, soft tube end first. For each side of the fly's tail, select three or four prime, 4 to 5" white saddle hackles and the same number of hot orange saddles. For a fuller finished fly, use more hackles.

Step 2: On each side of the tube, about 1/8" from the front edge of the hook holder, tie in the hackle butts, alternating the colors and splaying the feathers out in different directions.

Step 3: Cover the tied-in butts of the tail hackles with a palmered collar of large, webby orange and white saddle hackles. Use enough hackles to build a full, thick collar that stops 1/8" from the front end of the hard tube.

Step 4: Build a small, neat head, whip finish, and coat the wraps with cement.

Johnson Note: "When saltwater fly fishing pioneer Homer Rhode, Jr. wrote to Joseph Bates about this pattern in 1949, he said the splayed hackles improved the fly's action and that he tied them well back from the hook eye to avoid wrapping them around the shank. A short shank hook such as the Eagle Claw 253 maintains this advantage when the Rhode streamer is tied on a tube. According to Rhode, the hackles for the collar should be heavy and tightly wound. Bates quotes him in *Streamer Fly Tying and Fishing* as saying, 'I have found that these features cause fewer refusals, less mouthing of the tail—and I hook more and lose fewer fish.' Many successful saltwater patterns that have since been developed for Florida fishing retain the basic design characteristics of the early Homer Rhode streamer. This fly is effective in a great many solid and multiple color combinations."

A double limit of hatchery coho salmon caught in late August 1993 off Bush Point, Whidbey Island, Washington. Using the Calamarko tube fly and 5-weight outfits, Peter Harris and Mark Mandell caught and released 15 other salmon that evening. Mark Mandell photo

Garry Sandstrom (Tacoma, Washington)
Sandstrom Baitfish
Tied by Mark Mandell

Tubing: 1 3/4" of 1/8" hard plastic tubing, or brass, copper, or aluminum tubes (adjust the tube and wing lengths to match the size of the bait).
Thread: Clear monofilament thread and hot red thread.

Step 1: Put the plastic tube on your vise and attach the tying thread. Slip 1 7/8" of silver Mylar piping over front of the tube and adjust it so the end of the piping extends 3/4" past the end of the tube. With mono thread tie the piping down 1/4" from the rear end of the tube and whip finish. Tie it down at the head 1/2" from the front end with mono thread, whip finish, and Joli Glaze or Flexament the body and wraps. Let dry.

Step 2: Tie in a sparse 3" wing of polar bear or white FisHair. Tie in very small bunch of lime green Krystal Flash, the same length as the FisHair.

Step 3: Cut 1 1/2" of small pearlescent Mylar piping dyed lime green (see note below), remove and discard cotton core. Draw a line of Super Glue down the length of the piping, then let it dry completely. Cut the piping along the glue line. Fit the sheet of pearl lime green Mylar you've created to the underside of the head and wrap it down with a few turns of mono thread. Trim excess at nose and apply the rest of the sheet to the top of the head. Bind it with a few turns of thread as well. Trim the excess Mylar from around the back of the head.

Step 4: Tie in a piece of hot red thread at the back of the head, then wrap the piece of thread to make a neat red stripe around the head and in front of the wing—about 1/4 of the total head—then wrap it down with mono thread and trim excess red thread. Bind the head of the fly with mono thread, back to front, making the Mylar conform to its shape. Whip finish. Joli Glaze or epoxy head.

Mandell Note: "This is a tube version of a proven South Puget Sound salmon fly developed by Garry Sandstrom. (see Sandstrom's tube flies later in this chapter). If you can find Mylar piping in the color and size you need, obviously you don't have to go to the trouble of making a sheet and then binding it down. Just slide on the correctly-sized piping and wrap it down with mono thread."

Pat Trotter (Seattle, Washington)
Loligo II Squid
Tied by Mark Mandell

Tubing: 1 1/4" of 1/8" hard plastic or metal tubing and 1" of 3/16" vinyl tubing.
Thread: White Monocord.

Step 1: Dab Zap-a-Gap on one end of 1 1/4" of 1/8" hard plastic tubing and insert it into the vinyl tubing 3/4". Let dry. Paint a pair of large bead chain eyes white (or amber with black pupils). Let dry.

Step 2: Put the tube in your vise, vinyl end first. Start your tying thread about 1/2" from the back end of the tube. Select a pair of 3 1/2" white marabou blood feathers. Tie the marabou feathers to opposite sides of the tube, making wings 3" long. Trim the excess marabou and wrap down the butts securely.

Step 3: Pull off the fibers from pale pink, pale blue, and white hackle feathers. Mix the fibers, then tie in a thick bunch of them at the butts of the marabou. Rotate the tube in the vise as you do this, so the hackle fibers are distributed all around the tube.

Step 4: Mix up a dubbing made of two parts white and one part each of pale pink and pale blue fur or yarn. Wrap the dub-

bing forward 3/8" and stop. On top of the tube tie in the white bead chain eyes, securing them with figure-eights of thread. Then continue wrapping the dubbing forward another 3/8" and stop. At this point tie in together, butts first, two white saddle hackles, one pale pink, and one pale blue saddle hackle. Continue wrapping the dubbing forward to 1/4" from front end of tube and tie it down. Then wrap the four saddle hackles forward, tie them down, and trim the excess. Whip finish and cement wraps.

Ted Trueblood (Nampa, Idaho)
Integration
Tied by Mark Mandell

Tubing: 1" of 1/8" hard plastic tubing and 3/4" of 3/16" vinyl tubing.
Thread: Clear monofilament.

Step 1: Insert 1" of 1/8" hard plastic tubing into 3/4" of 3/16" vinyl tubing about 1/4", lining up the natural curves. Put the tube on your vise and tie down the join area with mono thread. Cut a sparse 2 1/2" bunch of pearl Flashabou. Tie it on top of tube, with the butts about 3/4" from the front of the tube. Apply slightly shorter bunches of pearl Flashabou to either side of the first, spread them out over the sides of the tube, and tie them down. Trim the excess Flashabou.

Step 2: Tie a sparse 3 1/2" white or polar bear FisHair wing on top of the longest bunch of Flashabou and top it with a few strands of pearl Krystal Flash. Trim the excess, whip finish and cement.

Step 3: Cut 2" of large white Everglow piping and slide it down over the front end of the tube until the tips of Everglow braid extend 1/4" past the end of the vinyl tubing. Tie the Everglow down at the nose with mono thread and wind the thread back over the head, binding the piping down, to the start of the wing. Cut off the excess hard plastic tubing and Everglow at the nose.

Step 4: Cut 1 1/2" of medium silver piping, remove and discard the core. Draw a line of Super Glue lengthwise down the Mylar piping, and let dry. Cut the silver piping along the glue line to form a sheet. Hold the sheet to the underside of the head and adjust its length so it covers about half of the underside of the vinyl tube as well as the underside of the head. Then trim the height of the Mylar so that when it's tied down it only covers the lower third of each side of the head. (You want the Everglow to show along the head's midline.) Tie down the Mylar, binding it to conform to the head shape. Trim the excess Mylar at the nose.

Step 5: Apply a very small amount of black FisHair on top of the white wing. The black wing should extend past the end of the head in front. Compress the black FisHair and wrap it down with mono thread to form a narrow black line along the center of the top of the head. Trim the excess FisHair from the tip of the nose.

Step 6: Tie in a couple of strands of silver Flashabou along each side of the white wing. Add two strands of black Flashabou to each side of head, tie them down, then space them with fingernail to give a striped effect. Add a few more wing-length strands of black Flashabou to the top of the head. Apply 7/32" silver Witchcraft eyes and tie down with two turns of mono thread. Whip finish. Trim the silver Mylar at throat into three spikes, the longest in the center. Coat with Joli Glaze or epoxy.

Mandell Note: "This is a tube version of one of the first flies used in Baja California saltwater."

Dave Whitlock (Tulsa, Oklahoma)
Whitlock Needlefish
Tied by Peter Harris

Tubing: 1 1/4" of 1/8" hard plastic tubing and 1" of 3/16" vinyl tubing.
Thread: Clear monofilament.

Step 1: Push 1/8" hard tubing into vinyl tubing 1/2". Put the tube on your vise and overwrap the join area with mono thread. Over the front of the tube slip a piece of medium pearl Mylar piping—it should extend past the back end of the tube about 1/2". Starting at the nose of the fly, overwrap the piping with mono to 1/4" from the back end of the tube. Advance the thread toward the tube's front end 1".

Step 2: Take a sparse 3 1/4" bunch of white FisHair, tapered to a point, and tie it on the top of the tube. Take two smaller bunches of white FisHair and tie them on either side of the first. FisHair should cover the top half of the back of the tube, and the underside of the tube should be FisHair-free.

Step 3: On top of the white FisHair tie a slightly longer bunch of lime green Krystal Flash. Make it long enough to reach

the nose of the tube. Overwrap it with mono thread from the nose to within 1/2" of the back of the tube, so it makes the top half of the tube light green.

Step 4: On top of the green Krystal Flash, tie in a slightly longer but sparser bunch of black Krystal Flash. Again make it long enough to reach the nose of the tube. Overwrap it with mono so it forms a black stripe down the center of the head. Tie in sparse bunches of pearl Flashabou 1/2" shorter than the white FisHair on either side of the fly.

Step 5: Smoothly taper the head at the join of the two sizes of tubing with wraps of mono thread. Apply 7/32" silver Witchcraft eyes on either side of head, wrap with mono, and whip finish. Or glue on 6mm doll's eyes and epoxy the head.

STREAMER TUBE FLIES

The streamers that follow are not adaptations of conventional patterns; they were designed specifically as tube flies, and are tied by their originators unless otherwise indicated.

Les Johnson working on a Baja dorado. Mark Mandell photo

Wally Adams (Renton, Washington)
Snow Creek Sand Lance

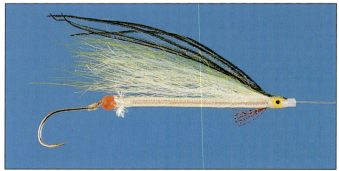

Tubing: 3" of 1/8" hard plastic tubing.
Thread: Clear monofilament.

Step 1: Slip a length of pearl Mylar piping over the plastic tube. Secure the piping at the rear of the tube with monofilament thread, tie off and complete with dab of Dave's Flexament.

Step 2: Tie in an underwing of sparse white polar bear hair, FisHair, or Super Hair.

Step 3: Tie in a top wing of medium green polar bear hair, FisHair, or Super Hair.

Step 4: On either side of the wing, tie in several strands of pearl Krystal Flash.

Step 5: Just above the Krystal Flash add a few strands of pearl Flashabou.

Step 6: Tie in four strands of peacock herl as a topping.

Step 7: Rotate the fly 180° on your vise and tie in several strands of red Krystal Flash as a throat.

Step 8: Complete the head with clear monofilament thread. Apply Dave's Flexament.

Step 9: Paint on yellow eyes with black pupils.

Adams Note: "I usually fish this pattern with a single salmon bait hook, using a red bead as a bearing surface between the end of the tube and the hook. This fly has taken cohos from Puget Sound in Washington to estuarine waters in Alaska."

Flashabou or Super Hair, slightly longer than the tube. Over this midwing, add several strands of pearl Krystal Flash.

Step 5: Top that with eight strands of peacock herl about 1" longer than the blue midwing.

Step 6: Whip finish the head and add eyes, either painted, Witchcraft or doll eyes, white with a black pupil. Complete the head with Dave's Flexament or epoxy.

Bale Note: "I'm not claiming any originality for this fly except to say that for some reason the color combination seems to be something special. I first used it years ago in the Queen Charlottes for mature coho, mostly in estuarine situations. Since then I've fished it trolling, dead drifted, or stripped fast and slow and have taken all species of salmon; chum, coho, chinook and sockeye. It has caught a 42-pound chinook in Alaska and 15-inch feeding coho in Oregon. It has also attracted lingcod, halibut, trevally and ladyfish. I generally like it in larger sizes than smaller, between four and five inches long. The pattern has changed little since I tied the first one years ago."

Marc Bale (Bellevue, Washington)
Bale Tube Fly

Tubing: 3" of 1/8" hard plastic tubing.
Thread: Yellow for securing piping on tube; red for the remainder and for finishing off the head.

Step 1: Slip a piece of yellow Day-Glo Mylar piping over the tube. Secure the Mylar with thread at both ends.

Step 2: Tie a sparse bunch of white polar bear, bucktail, Flashabou or Super Hair on top of tube. Rotate the tube 180° on the vise, making this the belly of the fly.

Step 3: Tie in a bunch of white polar bear, bucktail, Flashabou or Super Hair, approximately the same length of the tube. Over this base wing, add six strands of white Day-Glo Flashabou.

Step 4: Tie in a bunch of pale blue polar bear, bucktail,

Joe Butorac (Arlington, Washington)
Pipeline Special

This billfish streamer is made with the same materials and in the same steps as the Pop-Eyed Popper described in the "Basic Tying Steps" chapter. The only difference is, after you've tied on the largest of the turquoise saddle hackles in **Step 11**, you build up a long, smoothly tapered head with thread, and whip finish. Use a felt marker to color the dorsal side of head a matching blue, and epoxy the head. Then paint on yellow eyes with black pupils.

Butorac Note: "This billfish streamer is actually a tube version of an earlier, hook-tied fly of mine, the Sailfish Special. I also tie it in all-white, pink and white, green and yellow, red and white, green and white, red and pink, blue and pink, and yellow and white, and in smaller sizes for smaller fish."

Flasher Fly

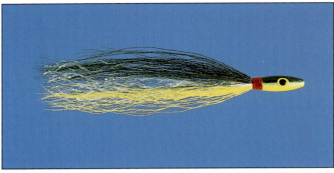

Tubing: 1/2" of 1/8" hard plastic tubing inserted into a molded, pre-painted (green and chartreuse, with yellow and black eyes) plastic head from Trophy Tackle, 5/8" long, 1/4" in diameter. The fly is dressed on the collar at the back of the slider head.

Thread: Size A rod winding thread in red.

Step 1: Put the connected molded head and hard tubing on your vise with the side of the head facing up and attach the thread just behind the join. Cut a 3" piece of small pearl Mylar piping and remove the core. Slip the piping over the back end of the tube and tie it down securely at the collar, only. Unravel and comb out the piping to the thread wraps.

Step 2: Turn the tube so the chartreuse side of the head is facing up. On the collar only, tie in a sparse 3" wing of chartreuse bucktail.

Step 3: Rotate the tube 180° and tie in a matching wing of dark green bucktail, on the collar, only.

Step 4: Whip finish and cement.

Butorac Note: "The Flasher Fly is the most popular commercially tied salmon tube fly in Puget Sound. The Trophy Slider (see Tube Poppers and Sliders chapter) is a Baja variation of this fly."

Flashy Lady

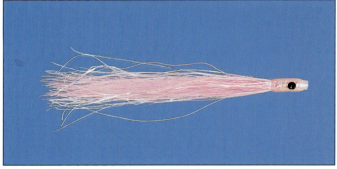

Tubing: 1/2 to 1" of 1/8" hard plastic tubing (slightly longer than the desired head) with the rear end cut at a 45° angle.

Thread: Clear monofilament.

Step 1: Attach the tying thread at about the middle of the tube. Tie in a sparse layer of 3" pink bucktail, 360° around the tube. The butt ends of the bucktail should extend past the front end of the tube. Wrap over the butt ends of the bucktail, forming the size and shape of the fly head. The clear thread allows the color of the bucktail to show through.

Step 2: Cut a piece of pearl Mylar piping to match the overall length of the fly. Remove the core. Slip one end of the piping over the fly head, leaving the majority of its length facing forward, and tie it down at the nose. Wind the thread back over the head to the collar.

Step 3: Unravel 3/4 of the forward-facing piping and pull it back over itself, Thunder Creek style.

Step 4: Tie down the piping at the collar. Whip finish.

Step 5: Apply epoxy or three coats of head cement to the head. Paint on black eyes.

Butorac Note: "This is the second most popular salmon tube fly in Puget Sound. I tie it in blue, yellow, and green and white, using a two-color wing on large sizes."

Coho Special

Tubing: 1/2 to 1" of 1/8" hard plastic tubing.

Thread: Clear monofilament.

Step 1: Attach the tying thread about the middle of the tube. Cut a 3" piece of small pearl Mylar piping and remove the core. Slip the piping over the back end of the tube and tie it down securely. Unravel and comb out the piping to the thread wraps.

Step 2: On top of the tube, tie in a wing of a medium bunch of 3" long white bucktail. It should extend forward the length of the head desired. Bind it down almost to the nose of the fly with monofilament.

Step 3: Rotate the tube 180° and tie in a second wing, same length and volume, made up of dark green bucktail. It should extend forward the length of the head desired. Bind it down with thread to the nose.

Step 4: Add eight to ten strands of pink Krystal Flash, same length as the wings, along the sides to simulate a lateral line. This should extend past the end of the tube in front, forming a stripe down the center line of the head. Bind it down with thread.

Step 5: Trim the excess tube from the front of the fly with a razor blade, make a neat head with thread, and whip finish.

Step 6: Epoxy the head, or give it three coats of thick head cement, then paint on yellow eyes with black pupils.

Krystal Fish

Tubing: 1/2 to 1" of 1/8" hard plastic tubing.
Thread: Clear monofilament.

Step 1: Start the tying thread at about the middle of the tube. Tie in a very sparse layer of 3 3/4" white or yellow bucktail or 24 Denier FisHair 360° around the tube.

Step 2: On top of the tube, tie in a bunch of pearl Krystal Flash. It should be slightly larger in volume, but exactly the same length as the bucktail or FisHair (the wing on this fly is not tapered), and it should extend forward the length of the head desired. With your thumbnail spread the pearl Krystal Flash to cover the top half of the tube and bind it down with monofilament.

Step 3: Rotate the tube 180° and tie in a second wing made up of 3/4 lime green, topped with 1/4 peacock green Krystal Flash. It, too, should extend forward the full length of the head. Tie it down with monofilament thread.

Step 4: Add a few strands of pink Krystal Flash along the sides to simulate a lateral line.

Step 5: Trim the excess Krystal Flash from the front of the tube, make a neat head with thread, and whip finish.

Step 6: Epoxy the head, or give it three coats of thick head cement, then paint on yellow eyes with black pupils.

Butorac Note: "To create a head-dropping motion on the retrieve, wrap the tube with lead fuse wire before tying on the Krystal Flash in **Step 2**. I also tie this fly with a blue, peacock, black, brown, red, and pink Krystal Flash wing."

Steve Damm (Bainbridge Island, Washington)
Needle Fly

Tubing: 3/4" of 1/8" hard plastic tubing, 3/4" of 3/16" vinyl tubing for a hook holder.
Thread: Clear monofilament.

Step 1: Start the mono thread on the soft tubing, a bit back from its front edge. Tie in enough mixed 2 to 2 3/4" lengths of pearl Flashabou to completely surround the tube in a very sparse, and somewhat ragged layer.

Step 2: Rotate the tube in your vise so the bottom side is up. Tie in a few strands of 3" long silver Flashabou.

Step 3: Rotate the tube 180° and tie in a super sparse layer of 3" long white FisHair completely around the tube.

Step 4: On top of the tube tie in an underwing consisting of a few strands of chartreuse FisHair, topped by a slightly heavier bit of green Ocean Hair, topped by a few strands of blue Ocean Hair. The forward portion of this extremely sparse wing should extend over the nose of the fly. Bind this down with mono to form a narrow dorsal stripe.

Step 5: Rotate the tube 180° in your vise and tie in a small bunch of red Krystal Flash at the throat. Clip short.

Step 6: Rotate the tube 180° and tie in a wing topping of 3 strands of black Flashabou. This is also bound down to form a dorsal stripe.

Step 7: Trim the excess materials. Stick on Witchcraft eyes, secure them with a turn of thread, and whip finish. Epoxy the head. When the epoxy is dry, trim away the excess hard tubing with a razor blade.

Baby Needlefish

Tubing: 1/2" of 1/8" hard plastic tubing.
Thread: Clear monofilament.

Step 1: Start the mono thread in the middle of the tube. Tie in enough 2" white FisHair to completely surround the tube in a very sparse, tapered layer.

Step 2: Take about a dozen 1 1/4" strands of pearl Krystal Flash and tie them in so they are spread evenly, 360° around the tube.

Step 3: On top of the tube tie in about a dozen strands of 1 3/4" chartreuse FisHair. Top this with three strands of black Krystal Flash, same length. Top that with three strands of pearl Krystal Flash, same length. The forward portion of this extremely sparse wing should extend over the nose of the fly. Bind this down with mono to form a narrow dorsal stripe.

Step 4: Form a small neat head with thread and whip finish. Paint small yellow eyes with black pupils. Epoxy the head. When the epoxy is dry, trim away the excess hard tubing with a razor blade.

Damm Note: "I use these two Needlefish flies for Puget Sound beach fishing. They are intended to mimic the tiny, almost transparent, immature baitfish that school in very shallow, very clear water. They have been successful on coho and blackmouth salmon and sea-run cutthroat."

Summer Fling

Tubing: 3/4" of 1/8" hard plastic tubing, 3/4" of 3/16" vinyl tubing for a hook holder.
Thread: Clear monofilament.

Step 1: Start the mono thread on the soft tubing, a bit back from its front edge. Tie in enough 2" long pearl Flashabou to completely surround the tube in a very sparse layer.

Step 2: Apply a very sparse layer of white FisHair, slightly longer than the Flashabou, completely around the tube.

Step 3: On top of the tube, tie in a very sparse underwing of chartreuse bucktail or FisHair. The forward portion should extend over the nose of the fly. Bind this down with mono to form a narrow chartreuse dorsal stripe.

Step 4: Apply a very sparse overwing of hot pink bucktail or FisHair. The forward portion should extend over the nose of the fly. Bind this down with mono to form a narrow hot pink dorsal stripe on top of the chartreuse.

Step 5: Form a small head with thread and whip finish. Paint small yellow eyes with black pupils. Epoxy the head. When the epoxy is dry, trim away the excess hard tubing with a razor blade.

Damm Note: "This fly is designed for fishing estuaries for pink salmon. I got the idea for the color combination (hot pink and yellow) from an article by Pat Trotter on conventional streamer flies for this species."

Dick Goin (Port Angeles, Washington)

Dick Goin took this bright summer-run steelhead in the tidewater section of the Olympic Peninsula's Quillayute River. Dick Goin photo

Dick Goin started tying freshwater tube flies in the early 1950s. His inspiration came from watching Port Angeles commercial tube tier Lloyd Peters at work on salmon trolling flies. Over the years, Dick has experimented with different types of tubes, including bird quills. Currently, he is using very fine (3/64" O.D.) clear plastic tubing he obtained through an instrument technician at the local paper mill. On this slender stuff, Dick ties small flies which he fishes on light tippets for steelhead in the rivers near his home. For a mandrel he uses a fine sewing needle. Dick has done some comparative fishing with hook-tied steelhead flies and his steelhead tubes, and believes that tube flies double his strike-to-hook-up ratio.

Green Head

Tubing: 1" of plastic 3/64" O.D. instrument tubing.
Thread: Black.

Step 1: Put the tubing on your mandrel and attach the tying thread. On top of the rear end of the tube tie in a 3/4" long tuft of black marabou fibers for a tail.

Step 2: At the rear of the tube, tie in a soft black hackle, tip first, wet fly style.

Step 3: Tie in a length of fine black wool.

Step 4: Wind the wool forward to 1/4" from the front end of the tube, tie it off, and trim the excess.

Step 5: Palmer the hackle forward to the end of the wool, tie it off and trim the excess.

Step 6: Tie in a length of fine light green chenille and make two turns of it. Tie it off and trim the excess.

Step 7: Whip finish and cement the wraps.

Goin Note: "Fished on a floating line with a size 8 hook and an eight-pound tippet, this fly has taken steelhead from 36" to 40 1/8" in clear water."

Pale Pink Marabou

Tubing: 1" to 1 1/4" of plastic 3/64" O.D. instrument tubing.
Thread: Pink.

Step 1: Put the tubing on your mandrel and attach the tying thread. At the rear of the tube tie in a length of fine, pale pink chenille. Wind the chenille forward to make a body 5/8 to 3/4" long. Tie off the chenille, and trim the excess.

Step 2: On top of the tube tie in a bunch of 1" long pale pink marabou fibers for a wing.

Step 3: In front of the marabou, tie in a 1 1/4" long bunch of pale lavendar Krystal Flash.

Step 4: Make a small, neat head with thread, whip finish, and cement the wraps.

Goin Note: "I've been using this fly on Olympic Peninsula steelhead for about 15 years. I tie it small and fish it with size 6 to 10 hooks."

A beautiful, 14-pound Olympic Peninsula steelhead taken on a small tube fly. Dick Goin photo

Pete's Special

Tubing: 1" to 1 1/4" of plastic 3/64" O.D. instrument tubing.
Thread: Orange.

Step 1: Put the tubing on your mandrel and attach the tying thread. On top of the tube at the rear end, tie in a short tail of orange hackle fibers.

Step 2: Tie in a length of orange wool. Wind the thread forward to midbody. Wind the orange wool to midbody, tie it off, and trim the excess.

Step 3: Tie in a length of fluorescent yellow wool. Wind the yellow wool forward to complete the body. Tie it down and trim the excess.

Step 4: Tie in a soft orange saddle hackle, wet fly style, and wrap several turns to make a collar. Tie the hackle off and trim the excess.

Step 5: On top of the tube tie in a tapered wing of white bucktail, about the same length as the body. Trim the excess.

Step 6: Whip finish and cement the wraps.

Goin Note: "This is a tube version of an old steelhead fly from the mid-1950s. It has worked very well for me."

Peter Harris
(Port Townsend, Washington and San Sebastian, Baja California Sur, Mexico)

Peter Harris kneels beside a pair of Sea of Cortez yellowtail taken on his Blunderbuss fly. Peter Harris photo

The Blunderbuss series of flies are all built on a plastic "golf tee." This isn't the same tee used in the game of golf. It's a cone-shaped and perforated piece of plastic (the funnel part of a real golf tee) that's meant to be inserted into the heads of vinyl squid or Hoochie type fishing lures to give them shape. It ends in a nipple rather than a spike.

Blunderbuss Squid/Shrimp

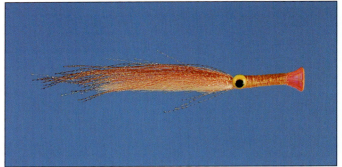

Tubing: 1 1/4" of 1/8" hard plastic tubing and 1 1/2" of fluorescent red 1/4" vinyl tubing.

Thread: Clear mono.

Step 1: Cut the nipple off a fluorescent red golf tee. Drill an 1/8" diameter hole through the center of the cone. Cut 1 1/4" of 1/8" hard plastic tubing and Super Glue it into the hole you've drilled so one end is flush with the bottom of the inside of the tee's funnel and the other protrudes out the back. Slip a 1 1/2" piece of fluorescent red 1/4" vinyl tubing over the protruding plastic tubing and push it up against the back (cut edge) of the tee. The overall length of the tee and tubing is 1 7/8". With clear mono thread, wrap over the red tubing, leaving about 1/4" uncovered at the back for a hook holder.

Step 2: Slip a 2" piece of medium pearlescent Mylar piping over the back end of the tube and push it up to the flare of the tee. Starting at the join between tee and tubing, wrap the piping down with mono thread to within 1/2" of the back end of the tube. Advance the thread toward the tube's front end 1".

Step 3: Take a 2 3/4" bunch of white FisHair, tapered to a point, and tie it on the side of the tube. Take an equal amount of white FisHair and tie it on the other side. The bunches of FisHair should form a slight hollow where they meet on top, and the underside of the tube should have no FisHair on it.

Step 4: Take a bunch of lavendar Krystal Flash slightly longer than the FisHair and tie it on top of the tube, so it fills the hollow between the two bunches of wing. Spread out the lavendar Krystal Flash so only a little of the white side of the wings is uncovered at the bottom on both sides.

Step 5: Lay a bunch of red Krystal Flash, tapered to a point, on top of the tube. It should be long enough to extend from the start of the flare of the funnel to 1 1/4" past the end of the white FisHair—about 4 3/4" overall. Tie down the red Krystal Flash with mono thread at the start of the flare of the funnel and spread it out to cover the top half of the tube. Overwrap the Krystal Flash with mono thread, then whip finish.

Step 6: With Super Glue, Flexament or Goop, glue 6mm yellow doll's eyes to the sides of the head, 7/8" from the start of the flare. Five-minute epoxy the whole head.

Harris Note: "I got the idea for this series of saltwater flies from a freshwater bass lure. When fished on the surface with a fairly brisk retrieve, the golf tee nose makes these flies skitter and pop out of the water erratically. They are meant to mimic an injured or panicked bait."

Blunderbuss Baitfish

Tubing: 1" of 1/8" hard plastic tubing and 1 1/4" of 1/4" clear vinyl tubing.

Thread: Clear monofilament.

Step 1: Cut the nipple off a clear tee. Drill an 1/8" diameter hole through the center of the cone. Cut 1" of 1/8" hard plastic tubing and Super Glue it into the hole you've drilled. One end of the tubing should be flush with the bottom of the inside of the tee's funnel and the other end of it protrudes out the back. Slip a 1 1/4" piece of clear 1/4" vinyl tubing over the protruding plastic tubing and push it up against the back (cut edge) of the tee. Overall length of tee and tubing is 1 1/2". With clear mono thread, wrap over the clear tubing, leaving about 1/4" uncovered at the back for a hook holder.

Step 2: Slip 1 1/2" of medium pearlescent Mylar piping over the back end of the tube and push it up to the flare of the tee. Starting at the join between tee and tubing, wrap the piping down with mono thread to within 1/2" of the back end of the tube. Advance the thread toward the tube's front end 1".

Step 3: Take a 2 3/4" bunch of white FisHair, tapered to a point, and tie it on the top of the tube. Take a smaller amount of white FisHair and tie it on either side of the first. The FisHair should cover the top half of the back of the tube, and the underside of the tube should have no FisHair on it.

Step 4: Tie a bunch of lavendar Flashabou, slightly shorter than the FisHair, on either side of the tube. Tie a bunch of lavendar Krystal Flash on top of the wing. It should be slightly longer than the wing.

Step 5: Lay a bunch of peacock colored Krystal Flash, tapered to a point, on top of the tube. It should be long enough to extend from the start of the flare of the funnel to 1 1/2" past the end of the white FisHair—about 5" overall. Tie down the peacock colored Krystal Flash with mono thread at the start of the flare of the funnel and spread it out to cover the top half of the tube. Overwrap the Krystal Flash with mono thread.

Step 6: Apply 7/32" silver Witchcraft eyes to sides of head about 3/4" back from start of flare, overwrap them with mono, then whip finish. Five-minute epoxy the whole head.

A trumpetfish fooled by a tube fly in a shallow, protected bay south of Mulege, Baja California. Les Johnson photo

Blunderbuss Corneta (Trumpetfish)
Tied by Mark Mandell

Tubing: 1 1/4" of 1/8" hard plastic tubing and 1 1/2" of 1/4" fluorescent green vinyl tubing.
Thread: Clear monofilament.

Step 1: Cut the nipple off a fluorescent green golf tee. Drill an 1/8" diameter hole through the center of the cone. Cut 1 1/4" of 1/8" hard plastic tubing and Super Glue it into the hole you've drilled. One end of the tube should be flush with the bottom of the inside of the tee's funnel and the other end protrudes out the back. Slip a 1 1/2" piece of fluorescent green 1/4" vinyl tubing over the protruding plastic tubing and push it up against the back (cut edge) of the tee. Overall length of tee and tubing is 2". With clear mono thread, wrap over the green tubing, leaving about 1/4" uncovered at the back for a hook holder.

Step 2: Slip 2 1/4" of medium pearlescent Mylar piping over the back end of the tube and push it up to the flare of the tee. Starting at the join between tee and tubing, wrap the piping down with mono thread to within 1/2" of the back end of the tube. Advance the thread toward the tube's front end 1".

Step 3: Then take a 2 3/4" bunch of white FisHair, tapered to a point, and tie it on the top of the tube. Take a smaller amount of white FisHair and tie it on either side of the first. The FisHair should cover the top half of the tube, and the underside of the tube should have no FisHair on it.

Step 4: Take a sparse bunch of lime green Krystal Flash slightly longer than the FisHair and tie it on top of the tube. Tie a slightly longer, but equally sparse bunch of aqua green Krystal Flash on top of the lime green.

Step 5: Lay about ten strands of combination silver/blue/green Flashabou on top of the tube. It should be long enough to extend from the start of the flare of the funnel to just past the ends of the Krystal Flash—about 4 1/2" overall. Tie down the Flashabou with mono thread at the start of the flare of the funnel and spread it out and overwrap with mono so it covers the top half of the tube all the way to the start of the wing. Then take about eight strands of black Flashabou the same length as the silver/green/blue and tie them down at the start of the flare. Overwrap the black with mono thread to form a neat stripe down the center of the head all the way back to the start of the wing.

Step 6: Apply 7/32" silver Witchcraft eyes to sides of head about 1" back from the start of the flare, overwrap them with mono, then whip finish. Five-minute epoxy the whole head.

This gorgeous Baja yellowtail snapper (pargo amarillo) hit a ".38 Special Calamarko." Les Johnson photo

Pink Calamarko

This is Peter Harris' version of Mark Mandell's Calamarko. See also Calamarko.
Tubing: 3/4" of 1/8" hard plastic tubing and 1" of 1/4" fluorescent red vinyl tubing.
Thread: Clear monofilament.

Step 1: Push 1/8" hard plastic tubing into 1/4" red vinyl tubing 1/2". Put the tube on your vise and overwrap the join area with mono thread. Tie a very sparse, tapered bunch of white FisHair on top of the tube. It should be as long as the tube in front and extend 3" past the back end of the tube. Wrap the FisHair down with mono thread from the nose of the fly to 1/4" from the rear end of the red tubing.

Step 2: Top this with a sparse, tapered, slightly longer bunch of hot pink FisHair. Wrap this down to the nose of the tube as in **Step 1**.

Step 3: On top of the FisHair tie a slightly longer and even sparser bunch of red Krystal Flash. The red Krystal Flash should also cover the entire length of the top side of the tube. Wrap it down as with the FisHair.

Step 4: On one side of the fly tie in a very sparse bunch of pearl Flashabou. It should be slightly shorter than the pink FisHair wing at the back, and as long as the tube in front. Below this, tie in a matching bunch of pearl Krystal Flash, the same length.

Step 5: Repeat **Step 4** for the other side of the tube. Tie down the material with mono to the nose and whip finish.

Step 6: Over the front of the tube slide on a piece of medium pearl Mylar piping—it should extend past the back end of the tube about 1/2". Starting at the nose of the fly, overwrap the piping with mono to 1/4" from the back end of the tube.

Step 7: Apply 7/32" silver Witchcraft eyes to the sides of the head 3/8" from the nose of the fly and overwrap them with mono. Five-minute epoxy the head.

Harris Note: "Like the original Calamarko, this fly has worked well on 'non-Gucci,' inshore Baja fish: striped pargo, yellowtail snapper, triggerfish, cabrilla, etc., etc."

Rudi Heger (Siegsdorf, Germany)

Rudi Heger releases a Dean River steelhead buck that fell to his black tube leech. Rudi Heger photo

Rudi Heger has been fishing the River Traun that runs next to his house in Siegsdorf, Germany since he was a child. A fly fisher and tier for more than 20 years, he started turning his passion for the sport into a business in 1980; since 1989, the running of Traun River Products (see Materials, Tools, Rigging chapter) has been his full-time occupation. Rudi is an avid seeker of big fish on a fly rod. He makes an annual pilgrimage to the blue ribbon steelhead waters of British Columbia, and also pursues saltwater tarpon, bonefish, and permit in Florida and Mexico. Rudi began developing the two series' of tube flies shown below in 1992. The first series has proven successful on pike, Atlantic barracuda, and huchen; the second was designed for British Columbia steelhead.

White and Gray

Tubing: 1 1/2" of 1/8" aluminum.
Thread: White 6/0.

Step 1: Put 1 1/2" of 1/8" aluminum tubing on your vise. Start your thread 3/8" from the back end of the tube. On top of the tube, tie in a sparse bunch of 2" long white bucktail. Rotate the tube 180° and tie in a matching bunch of 2" long white bucktail. Rotate the tube 90° and tie in a third bunch of white bucktail, the same length. Rotate the tube 180° and tie in a final bunch of white bucktail, the same length.

Step 2: Between the top pair of white bucktail bunches, tie in a thick bunch of 2" long white marabou fibers. Rotate the tube on your vise and tie in a second bunch of marabou between the next pair of bucktail bunches. Rotate the tube and tie in bunches of marabou in between the third, then the fourth pairs of bucktail bunches. When you're done, the rear of the tube should be encircled with marabou and bucktail. Wrap down the marabou and bucktail butts and return the thread to the starting point.

Step 3: At the thread starting point, on top of the tube, tie in two 5" strands of pearl Krystal Flash. Rotate the tube 180° and tie in two more strands. Rotate the tube 90° and tie in two more strands. Rotate the tube 180° and tie in two more strands.

Step 4: At the thread starting point tie in pearl Spectraflash chenille and advance thread to front of tube. Wind the chenille forward to 5/8" from the front end of the tube, tie off, and trim the excess.

Step 5: At the front of the tube, over the strands of Krystal Flash, tie in a sparse bunch of 3" white bucktail. Rotate the tube 90° and tie in a sparse bunch of 3" gray bucktail. Rotate the tube 90° and tie in sparse bunch of 3" white bucktail. Rotate the tube 90° and tie in a sparse bunch of 3" gray bucktail. Trim the excess.

Step 6: Over the topmost gray bucktail wing, tie in a dozen 5 1/2" strands of gold/blue Spectraflash Hair (Flashabou Tinselflash). Rotate the tube 90° and on top of the white wing tie in a dozen strands of 5 1/2" of gold/blue Spectraflash. Rotate 90° and tie in another bunch of gold/blue Spectraflash Hair. Rotate 90° and tie in a last bunch of Spectraflash.

Step 7: Build a neatly tapered head with thread, whip finish and cement. Paint head with gray lacquer.

A large freshwater pike poses with a tube fly outside its powerful jaws. Rudi Heger photo

All Brown

Tubing: 1 1/2" of 1/8" aluminum.
Thread: Brown 6/0.

Step 1: Put 1 1/2" of 1/8" aluminum tubing on your vise. Start your thread 3/8" from the back end of the tube. On top of the tube, tie in a sparse bunch of 2" long, light-tipped brown bucktail. Rotate the tube 180° and tie in a matching bunch of 2" long bucktail. Rotate the tube 90° and tie in a third bunch of bucktail, the same length. Rotate the tube 180° and tie in a final bunch of bucktail, the same length.

Step 2: Between the top pair of bucktail bunches, tie in a thick bunch of 2" long brown marabou fibers. Rotate the tube on your vise and tie in a second bunch of marabou between the next pair of bucktail bunches. Rotate the tube and tie bunches of marabou in between the third, then the fourth pairs of bucktail bunches. When you're done, the rear of the tube should be encircled with brown marabou and bucktail. Wrap down the marabou and bucktail butts and return the thread to the starting point.

Step 3: At the thread starting point, on top of the tube, tie in two 5" strands of brown Krystal Flash. Rotate the tube 90° and tie in two more strands. Rotate the tube 90° and tie in two more strands. Rotate the tube 90° and tie in two more strands.

Step 4: At the thread starting point tie in brown Spectraflash chenille and advance thread to front of tube. Wind the chenille forward to 5/8" from the front end of the tube, tie off, and trim the excess.

Step 5: At the front of the tube, over the strands of Krystal Flash, tie in a sparse bunch of 3" light brown bucktail. Rotate the tube 90° and tie in a sparse bunch of 3" light brown bucktail. Rotate the tube another 90° and tie in a sparse bunch of 3" light brown bucktail. Rotate the tube another 90° and tie in a last bunch of matching bucktail.

Step 6: Over the topmost brown bucktail wing, tie in a dozen 5 1/2" strands of copper Spectraflash Hair (Flashabou Tinselflash). Tie in equal amounts of copper Spectraflash on top of the other three wings.

Step 7: Build a neatly tapered head with thread, whip finish and cement. Paint head with brown lacquer.

Blue and Gray

Tubing: 1 1/2" of 1/8" aluminum.
Thread: White 6/0.

Step 1: Put 1 1/2" of 1/8" aluminum tubing on your vise. Start your thread 3/8" from the back end of the tube. On top of the tube, tie in a sparse bunch of 2" long gray bucktail. Rotate the tube 180° and tie in a matching bunch of 2" long gray bucktail. Rotate the tube 90° and tie in a third bunch of gray bucktail, the same length. Rotate the tube 180° and tie in a final bunch of gray bucktail, the same length.

Step 2: Between the top pair of gray bucktail bunches, tie in a thick bunch of 2" long gray marabou fibers. Rotate the tube on your vise and tie in a second bunch of marabou between the next pair of bucktail bunches. Rotate the tube and tie bunches of marabou in between the third, then the fourth pairs of bucktail bunches. When you're done, the rear of the tube should be encircled with marabou and bucktail. Wrap down the marabou and bucktail butts and return thread to the starting point.

Step 3: At the thread starting point, on top of the tube, tie in two 5" strands of pearl Krystal Flash. Rotate the tube 90° and tie in two more strands. Repeat this same procedure two more times.

Step 4: At the thread starting point tie in gray Spectraflash chenille and advance the thread to the front of tube. Wind the chenille forward to 5/8" from the front end of the tube, tie off, and trim the excess.

Step 5: At the front of the tube, over the strands of Krystal Flash, tie in a sparse bunch of 3" light blue bucktail. Rotate the tube 90° and tie in a sparse bunch of 3" gray bucktail. Rotate the tube 90° and tie in sparse bunch of 3" light blue bucktail. Rotate the tube 90° and tie in a sparse bunch of 3" gray bucktail.

Step 6: Over the topmost gray bucktail wing, tie in a dozen strands of 5 1/2" light blue Spectraflash Hair (Flashabou Tinselflash). Rotate the tube 90° and on top of the light blue wing tie in a dozen strands of 5 1/2" of gold/blue Spectraflash. Rotate the tube 90° and tie in another bunch of light blue Spectraflash Hair on the second gray wing. Again rotate 90° and tie in a last bunch of gold/blue Spectraflash on the other light blue wing.

Step 7: Build a neatly tapered head with thread, whip finish and cement. Paint the head with blue lacquer.

A Dean River, British Columbia, hen steelhead and the black tube leech that drew her strike. Note the dressed single hook in the fish's mouth and the free sliding tube fly below. Rudi Heger photo

All Black

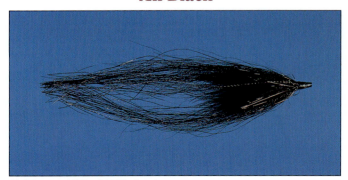

Tubing: 1 1/2" of 1/8" aluminum.
Thread: Black 6/0.

Step 1: Put 1 1/2" of 1/8" aluminum tubing on your vise. Start your thread 3/8" from the back end of the tube. On top of

the tube, tie in a sparse bunch of 2" long black bucktail. Rotate the tube 180° and tie in a matching bunch of 2" long black bucktail. Rotate the tube 90° and tie in a third bunch of black bucktail, the same length. Rotate the tube 180° and tie in a final bunch of black bucktail, the same length.

Step 2: Between the top pair of black bucktail bunches, tie in a thick bunch of 2" long black marabou fibers. Rotate the tube on your vise and tie in a second bunch of marabou between the next pair of bucktail bunches. Rotate the tube and tie bunches of marabou in between the third, then the fourth pairs of bucktail bunches. When you're done, the rear of the tube should be encircled with marabou and bucktail. Wrap down the marabou and bucktail butts and return the thread to the starting point.

Step 3: At the thread starting point tie in purple Spectraflash chenille (see "Materials, Tools, Rigging" chapter) and advance thread to front of tube. Wind the chenille forward to 5/8" from the front end of the tube, tie off, and trim the excess.

Step 4: At the front of the tube, over the marabou, tie in a sparse bunch of 3 1/2" black bucktail. Rotate the tube 90° and tie in a second sparse bunch of 3 1/2" black bucktail. Repeat this procedure two more times.

Step 5: Over the topmost bucktail wing, tie in a dozen strands of 5 1/2" of black Spectraflash Hair (Flashabou). Tie equal bunches of black Spectraflash over the other three wings.

Step 6: On top of each of the four bunches of black Spectraflash, tie in six 5" strands of pearl Krystal Flash.

Step 7: Build a neatly tapered head with thread, whip finish and cement. Paint the head with black lacquer.

Heger Note: "Pike and huchen have one thing in common: they like to attack the front or middle portion of their prey. To get the best hooking results, I have centered the hook in the middle of these flies, extending the wings with very limp flash material that moves freely in the water. I designed these flies so they remain bulky when wet and do not collapse on the retrieve. I tie them on aluminum tubes because they are very stable and easy to tie on, durable, and have just the right weight to slowly sink, yet act very alive in the water. The All Black pattern has taken huchen to 32 pounds."

This 32-pound huchen was caught on a Rudi Heger All Black by Tino Brandl, Bad Toelz, Bavaria, Germany, in the River Isar. The huchen is a genus of strictly freshwater European salmonid with a range limited to the Danube River and certain of its tributaries. Huchen can reach weights of more than 60 pounds. Tino Brandl photo

Steelhead Shrimp-Tube Leech

Tubing: 1 1/2" of 1/8" aluminum, with a 1/2" long, 1/8" vinyl hook holder.
Thread: Red.

Step 1: Start the thread 1/4" from the rear end of the tube to leave room for the hook holder. Tie in hot pink chenille, wrap it forward five turns, and secure but do not trim it.

Step 2: Tie in a hot orange saddle hackle, wet fly style, and wind it in. Tie down and trim the excess feather.

Step 3: Advance the chenille another five turns, secure, but do not trim it.

Step 4: Repeat **Step 2**.

Step 5: Advance the chenille two or three more turns, tie it down, and trim the excess.

Step 6: Trim orange hackle fibers away from both sides of body.

Step 7: On top of the tube, tie in a wing of orange polar bear. It should extend to the ends of the rearmost hackle fibers.

Step 8: Rotate the tube 180° in your vise and repeat **Step 7**.

Step 9: On either side of the wing, tie in a few strands of pearl Krystal Flash, 3" long.

Step 10: On top of the wing, tie in eight strands of metallic red and purple multicolor Spectraflash (Flashabou), the same length as the Krystal Flash.

Step 11: Rotate the tube 180° and repeat **Steps 9** and **10**.

Step 12: Whip finish and apply head cement.

Heger Note: "This fly was very productive for me on the Dean (British Columbia) in 1994."

Les Johnson (Seattle, Washington)
Johnson Sand Lance

Tubing: 1" of 1/8" hard plastic tubing for a larger fly. For a smaller fly use a 1" plastic Slipstream tube.
Thread: Clear monofilament.

Step 1: Start the mono thread on the soft tubing, a bit back from its front edge. Tie in a few strands of pink FisHair or Super Hair to mark the top of the tube.

Step 2: Tie a sparse layer of pearl Flashabou on the top and sides of tube, leaving a slight gap at the bottom to accommodate hook.

Step 3: Tie in a sparse, tapered bunch of white FisHair or Super Hair on the top and sides of the tube.

Step 4: On top of the white FisHair base, tie in a sparse wing about 3/8" longer than the white, in three equal parts of olive green over light green over gray, tapering each color before tying it in.

Step 5: Down each side of fly, along the white wing base, tie in two strands of silver Krystal Flash, the same length as the wing.

Step 6: Top this with four strands of peacock herl extending to the end of the wing. Dark green, or June Bug Flashabou can be substituted for the peacock herl.

Step 7: Rotate the tube 180° on your vise. Tie in several strands of red or fluorescent orange Flashabou as a throat. Clip short.

Step 8: Stick on Witchcraft eyes, then secure them in place with a few turns of clear monofilament.

Step 9: Whip finish and cover head with a thin coat of epoxy.

Johnson Note: "This pattern has become a standby for me from the Queen Charlottes in British Columbia to Puget Sound in Washington. I use it year-round in lengths from two-and-a-half to four inches to match the size of the sand lance salmon, Dolly Varden and cutthroat are feeding on. Care must be taken when tying this pattern to keep it sparse as the sand lance is a very slim baitfish with an undulating swimming motion that can't be properly imitated with a heavily dressed tube."

Les Johnson revives a pink salmon, Queen Charlotte Islands, British Columbia. Trey Combs photo

Capitán Skippy's Chico Carnada

Tubing: 1 1/2" of 1/8" hard plastic tubing with 1 1/2" of 3/16" vinyl tubing as a hook holder. For a fast sinking pattern substitute a 1 1/2" copper tube for the hard plastic. The overall fly length is between four and seven inches.

Thread: White floss and clear monofilament.

Step 1: Start the white floss on the soft tubing, a bit back from its front edge. Tie in a very sparse bunch (three or four strands only) of pink FisHair to mark the top of the tube.

Step 2: Tie in a sparse, tapered layer of pearl Flashabou to cover each side of the tube.

Step 3: Develop a baitfish body shape with a sparse, tapered layer of white FisHair all the way around the tube, leaving a slight gap at the bottom to accommodate the hook.

Step 4: Tie in a medium sized, tapered bunch of white FisHair, on top of the tube to build body depth.

Step 5: Whip finish the white floss, trim the excess and tie in the clear monofilament.

Step 6: Tie in four strands of silver Krystal Flash down each side, the length of the body.

Step 7: On top, tie in a sparse, tapered bunch of mouse gray FisHair as a mid-wing.

Step 8: Tie in a sparse, tapered top wing using equal parts of blue, moss green and lime green FisHair, mixed.

Step 9: Tie in a few strands of June Bug Flashabou topped with a few strands of black Krystal Flash.

Step 10: Rotate the tube 180° on the vise and tie in a few strands of fluorescent orange Flashabou as a throat. Clip short.

Step 11: Stick on Witchcraft eyes, then secure them in place with a few turns of clear monofilament.

Step 12: Whip finish and cover the head with a thin coating of epoxy.

Johnson Note: "I use this pattern when fishing the Sea of Cortez from Mulege to Loreto. It is more effective offshore, in blue water, than in shallow green bays and is my personal favorite dorado fly. It is a reasonable imitation of the *sardina* (or anchovy), but is intended to be a small, basic baitfish, hence the name Chico Carnada (little baitfish). I use white floss instead of thread in the early tying steps for this pattern because it allows me to build a bulkier fly more quickly."

Capitán Skippy's Ghost Carnada

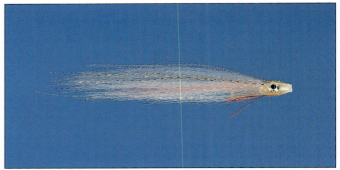

Tubing: 1 1/2" of 1/8" plastic tubing with 1 1/2" of 3/16" vinyl tubing for a hook holder.

Thread: Clear monofilament.

Step 1: Start the mono thread on the soft tubing, a bit back from its front edge. Tie in a few strands of pink Super Hair (three or four) to mark the top of the tube.

Step 2: Develop a baitfish body shape with a sparse, tapered layer of white Super Hair all the way around the tube, leaving a slight gap at the bottom to accommodate the hook.

Step 3: Add a sparse, tapered bunch of white Super Hair on top of the tube.

Step 4: Tie in two strands each of pearl and silver Krystal Flash down each side of body.

Step 5: Tie in a tapered wing, the same length as the white, made of sparse, equal parts of gray under pale blue Super Hair.

Step 6: Top it with a half dozen strands of lavendar Krystal Flash.

Step 7: Rotate the tube 180° on your vise and tie in a few strands of red or fluorescent orange Flashabou as a throat. Clip short.

Step 8: Stick on Witchcraft eyes, then secure them in place with a few turns of clear monofilament.

Step 9: Whip finish and cover the head with a thin coat of epoxy.

Johnson Note: "Over the sandy bottoms of shallow bays in Mexico, the Ghost Carnada, very translucent in the water because of the Super Hair, is a good producer on triggerfish, cabrilla, barred pargo and any other of the many species that haunt the shallow bays in late spring and early summer."

Capitán Skippy's Little Coho

Tube: 1 1/2" of 1/8" hard plastic tubing with 1 1/2" of vinyl tubing over the back as a hook holder. For a faster sinking fly use a 1 1/2" Slipstream tube in aluminum or brass.
Thread: White floss and clear monofilament.

Step 1: Using white floss, tie in a body of tapered white FisHair or Super Hair all the way around the tube, leaving a small gap at the bottom to accommodate the hook.

Step 2: On top of the tube, tie in an additional sparse bunch of white FisHair or Super Hair, slightly longer than the rest, to add bulk.

Step 3: Whip finish the white floss and trim the excess. Tie in clear monofilament thread.

Step 4: On top of the white FisHair or Super Hair, tie in a very sparse bunch of tapered violet FisHair or Super Hair.

Step 5: Tie in a sparse bunch of bright green FisHair or Super Hair on top of the violet.

Step 6: Tie in a sparse bunch of dark blue FisHair or Super Hair on top of the bright green.

Step 7: On each side of the fly tie in four strands of silver Flashabou, the same length as the white wing. On top of the Flashabou, tie in four strands of silver Krystal Flash, same length.

Step 8: On each side of the head, tie in a flattened, 3/4" section of silver Mylar piping that has been epoxied and cut to the shape of a baitfish's gill plate.

Step 9: On top of the fly, tie in several strands of silver Flashabou topped with several strands of black Krystal Flash, the same length as the wing. Wrap the black Krystal Flash down to the nose of the fly with mono thread, making a neat dorsal stripe.

Step 10: Rotate the tube 180° and tie in a half dozen strands of red Flashabou as a throat. Clip the Flashabou short.

Step 11: Rotate the tube 180° again. Stick on glow-in-the-dark Witchcraft eyes, and wrap them down with a turn or two of thread.

Step 12: Whip finish and coat the head with epoxy.

Johnson Note: "This pattern was designed primarily for salmon in Washington waters but has also worked well in Alaska and British Columbia. When tying this fly I usually prepare several sets of Mylar piping gills ahead of time by cutting up one-and-one-half inch lengths, removing the cores, and giving one end of the Mylar a coat of epoxy. When the epoxy has set up, I cut each piece to shape."

Les Johnson and guide with a dorado caught on one of Johnson's Chico Carnada tube flies, Loreto, Baja California. Bob Young Photo

Mike Kinney (Oso, Washington)

Mike Kinney, who makes his home not far from the Stillaguamish River, is a fly fishing guide and streamkeeper by trade and one of the most creative fly tiers in the Pacific Northwest. His fondness for classic salmon steelhead patterns is reflected in his own dressings which often include multi-feather wings and subtle colors. Although he ties most of his flies on hooks, Mike has begun dressing patterns on Waddington Shanks (see photo in "Atlantic salmon Tube Flies" chapter) and tubes, primarily to further his understanding of the fly tying art.

Dark Daze
(with dressed hook)

Tubing: 1 1/2" Slipstream plastic tube.
Thread: Purple 8/0 Danville.

Step 1: At the rear of the tube tie in a length of medium flat pearl Mylar tinsel, a length of purple Uni Yarn and a long, wispy purple saddle hackle by the tip. Wind the thread forward to 1/8" from the front of the tube.

Step 2: Wind the Uni Yarn forward evenly, and secure it.

Step 3: Wind the pearl Mylar tinsel forward four evenly-spaced turns, and secure it.

Step 4: Palmer the purple hackle forward between the ribbing wraps and secure it.

Step 5: Tie in a black saddle hackle, wet fly style, and wind four turns. Tie off and trim the excess hackle.

Step 6: Select two matching dyed purple pheasant rump feathers from opposite sides of the patch. Wet the feathers and draw them through your fingers. Tear away excess material from the bases of the stems until you have a good wing shape.

Step 7: Tie in the pheasant rump feathers, tent-style over body.

Step 8: Whip finish the head and cement.

Step 9: Select a hook of your choice (Mike used a treble here) to be dressed to match the tube.

Step 10: Tie in a purple saddle hackle at the rear of the hook shank, tip first, wet fly style.

Step 11: Make a dubbing loop and spin in a sparse amount of bright green SLF dubbing.

Step 12: Wind the dubbing forward and secure it. Palmer the hackle forward, tie it down and trim the excess.

Step 13: Whip finish and cement the wraps.

Kinney Note: "When steelhead have been in the river awhile and have seen a lot of flies, they tend to get wary. I've found that this is when the subtle color and movement of the Dark Daze works best. It has become one of my favorites for spooky fish and low, clear conditions."

Dan Lemaich (Camano Island, Washington)
Skagit River Winter Fly
(with dressed hook)

Tubing: 1 1/4" plastic Slipstream tube.
Thread: Danville 8/0 to match the fly.

Step 1: Tie in a length of flat silver Mylar tinsel at the front of the tube, wind it to the rear, then half way back up the tube, and secure it. Trim excess tinsel.

Step 2: Tie in a full marabou blood where the tinsel is tied off. Wrap the marabou forward, secure it and trim the excess.

Step 3: Repeat **Step 2** with another marabou the same, or a contrasting, color.

Step 4: Tie in a long, wispy saddle hackle, make four turns, then tie it off and trim the excess.

Step 5: Whip finish and cement the wraps.

Trailer Hook #1

Step 1: Select a hook of your choice for the trailer dressing.

Step 2: Tie in a length of flat or oval silver tinsel at the rear of the hook.

Step 3: Dub a body of SLF, then comb it out with a tooth brush.

Step 4: Tie in a bunch of marabou blood fibers, the length of the body, as a wing.

Step 5: Tie in a saddle hackle, wind four turns, secure it and trim the excess.

Step 6: Whip finish and cement the wraps.

Trailer Hook #2

Step 1: Same as for Trailer #1.

Step 2: Half way up the hook shank tie in a marabou blood by the tip. Palmer it forward and secure. Trim the excess.

Step 3: Tie in a second marabou blood and repeat **Step 3**.

Step 4: Tie in a contrasting saddle hackle and make four turns as a face. Tie off and trim the excess.

Step 5: Dub in a collar ahead of the hackle with contrasting SLF.

Step 6: Whip finish and cement the wraps.

Lemaich Note: "Using a tube dressing ahead of the fly has become popular over the past several years with many veteran fly fishers on the Skagit River for winter steelheading, particularly in dark or murky water. By adding a dressed tube ahead of the fly, you can present a large silhouette and still have a fly that can be cast with a one-handed rod. With a Spey rod it is possible to add two, or even three tubes ahead of a fly and present a huge dressing—and Skagit steelhead will not hesitate to hit it. Colors don't seem to matter. I keep a selection in my vest and mix or match them any way that suits me."

Mark Mandell and guide in 1994 with a bonito estimated at 22 pounds released after a 40 minute fight at the San Bruno shark nets, Sea of Cortez. Les Johnson photo

Mark Mandell (Port Townsend, Washington)
Calamarko

Tubing: 1" of 1/8" plastic tubing and 3/4" of 3/16" vinyl tubing for a hook holder. For deep fishing, substitute 1" of 1/8" brass or copper tubing for the 1/8" plastic.
Thread: Clear monofilament.

Step 1: Apply a drop or two of Zap-A-Gap to the outside of one end of the hard tube, then insert it into the vinyl tube about 1/2", matching the natural curves. Let dry. Put the tube on your vise, or insert a hook eye into the vinyl tubing and chuck the hook into a standard vise. Wrap the join area of the hard and soft tubing with a half dozen turns of clear mono thread, then wind thread to 1" from the back end of the vinyl tubing. Along the top of the tube (spine), tie in a sparse bunch of pearl Flashabou 3" long. Then tie a sparse bunch of 2" long pearl Flashabou on each side of the first, so by the time you're done the Flashabou thinly covers about half the top circumference of the tube, leaving the underside open.

Step 2: Tie in a sparse bunch of polar bear FisHair, 3 1/2" long and tapered to a point, on the spine. Sparse 3" to 3 1/4" bunches of FisHair go on either side of the first wing. Again, the underside of the fly is left uncovered. Tie in a few strands of pearl Krystal Flash, the same length as the side FisHair, on either side of the wing. Cement.

Step 3: Use mono thread to build a long, tapered head, and whip finish. Pull the core of some white medium Everglow piping out a few inches. Slip the Everglow over the fly head until the tips of the braid extend an inch or so beyond the back end of the vinyl tubing. Use several tight wraps of mono thread to tie down the Everglow at the nose. Cut off the excess hard tubing and Everglow at the nose (but don't cut the mono thread).

Step 4: Lay a dozen or so strands of purple Krystal Flash over the FisHair wing and adjust it so it's the same length or slightly longer. In front, it should extend past the end of the nose. Tie it down at the end of the nose with mono thread. Wrap the thread back so the Krystal Flash makes an even purple stripe along the top of the head to the start of the wing, about 3/4" back from the nose of the fly. Apply 5/32" Witchcraft eyes, gold or silver, to the sides of the head near the base of the wing and wrap over them with two turns of mono. If necessary, even up the head with more wraps of mono thread and whip finish. With a bobbin, fray out the back end of the Everglow piping to make a skirt. Cover the fly head just to the start of the wing with Joli Glaze or epoxy.

Mandell Note: "This fly was inspired by Mark Waslick's Sea Bait tube streamer, and is intended to represent an immature squid. It works as a cast fly or trolled. For a really deep sink, I sometimes wrap the brass tube with lead wire before tying on it. Les calls these '.38 Special Calamarkos.' We have used this fly in the Northwest saltwater for all species of salmon, and in smaller sizes—down to 2 1/2" overall length, tied on a hard plastic tube without a hook holder—for sea-run cutthroat. It has also been successful in Baja for all inshore species (see also, the Pink Calamarko). In both the Northwest and Baja I've seen Les Johnson stop fishing with this fly because he said it was too effective to be sporting."

Candlefish

Tubing: 1" of 1/8" hard plastic or metal tubing and 1 1/4" of 3/16" vinyl tubing.

Thread: Clear monofilament.

Step 1: Insert 1" of 1/8" hard plastic tubing into 1 1/4" of 3/16" vinyl tubing about 1/4", lining up the natural curves. Put the tube on your vise and tie down the join area with mono thread. Advance the thread to 1" from the end of the tube. Tie a sparse bunch of 3 1/4" long pearl Flashabou on top of the tube. On either side of this, tie in a 2 1/2" bunch of pearl Flashabou, spreading the fibers over the sides of the tube, but leaving the bottom bare.

Step 2: Add a sparse wing of 4" white or polar bear FisHair. Then lay a bunch of yellow Krystal Flash on top of the white wing. It should be slightly longer than the FisHair. Shoulder the fly on each side with a few strands of silver Flashabou, 3 1/4" long. Build a tapered head with mono thread. Whip finish and cement.

Step 3: Slide 2" of large white Everglow piping over the nose of the fly. Adjust the piping so the tips of the Everglow braid extend 1/4" past the end of the vinyl tubing. Bind the piping down over the head with mono thread.

Step 4: Trim the Everglow braid from over the wing. Top the wing with a sparse bunch of olive green FisHair 4 1/4" long. In front, it should extend past the end of the head. Compress the olive FisHair to make a green stripe down the center of the head and tie it down with mono thread.

Step 5: Top the olive FisHair with a few strands of lavendar Krystal Flash. Then tie in a few strands of yellow Krystal Flash next to the olive green FisHair on both sides of the head. Trim the excess yellow Krystal Flash at the nose and back of the head, making a neat yellow stripe on the head below the green dorsal line. Add 5/32" silver Witchcraft eyes and wrap them with two turns of thread, then whip finish. Trim excess material from nose of fly, then Joli Glaze or epoxy head.

Mandell Note: "At Mid-Channel Bank near my home, local anglers catch candlefish (sand lance) with dipnets and use them for salmon bait. Salmon taken at Mid-Channel usually have nothing but these fish in their stomachs. In handling hundreds of live sand lance over the last eight years, prior to packaging and freezing them for later use, I've noticed that some have a pronounced gold/yellow edge to their olive green dorsal. I tried to incorporate this into the head and wing of a Waslick Sea Bait-style fly."

Garry Sandstrom (Tacoma, Washington)

Garry Sandstrom holds a six-pound dorado taken on a 1-weight rod, Loreto, Baja California, Mexico. Garry Sandstrom photo

Garry Sandstrom is the owner of the Morning Hatch Fly Shoppe in Tacoma, Washington and has been a saltwater fly fisherman and innovative fly tier for 20 years. Garry was one of the first anglers to cast tube flies to Puget Sound chinook and coho salmon. He started designing and fishing tube flies in 1976, around the time the highly successful Puget Sound resident coho program was implemented. Garry has continued to develop tube flies for fresh and saltwater, and always carries tube flies with him to Alaska, British Columbia and the warm waters of Mexico.

Diamond Back - Coho

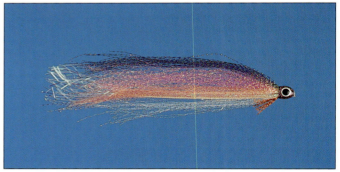

Tubing: 2 to 5" of 1/8" hard plastic tubing, depending on the size of the fly.

Thread: White Monocord.

Step 1: Slide a piece of small pearl Mylar piping over the plastic tube. Secure the piping with thread at both ends, tying it off flush with the front of the tube and leaving it a bit longer than the tube in back. After you've tied the piping down, unravel it at the rear to form a tail.

Step 2: On top of the tube tie in a sparse bunch of pearl Krystal Flash, the length of the body and tail. Add a short bunch of red Krystal Flash as a throat. Rotate the tube 180° on the vise so this becomes the belly of the fly.

Step 3: Tie in a sparse bunch of pink Krystal Flash, the length of the body and tail.

Step 4: Tie in sparse bunch of lavender Krystal Flash, the length of the body and tail.

Step 5: Top with a sparse bunch of purple Krystal Flash, the length of the body and tail.

Step 6: Complete the head with close turns of micro tinsel to match the color of the topping on the fly. Whip finish. Add painted eyes and cover the head with a light coat of epoxy.

Sandstrom Note: "I developed this fly after thinking that if a little Krystal Flash is good, why not use a whole bunch? At first I though it would be too flashy and spook the fish. Actually, it wound up outproducing my original bucktail models. You can use Krystal Flash, Flashabou Accent, or a combination of both for the Diamond Back patterns. Flashabou Accent seems to provide a bit thicker profile. I tie a variety of patterns based on this design."

Diamond Back - Dorado

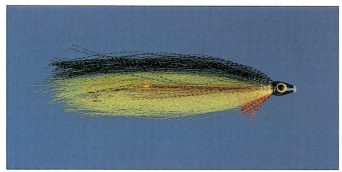

Tubing: 2" to 5" of 1/8" hard plastic tubing, depending on the size of the fly.
Thread: White Monocord.

Step 1: Slide a piece of small gold Mylar piping over the plastic tube. Secure the piping with thread at both ends, tying it off flush with the front of the tube and leaving it a bit longer than the tube in back. After you've tied the piping down, unravel it at the rear to form a tail.

Step 2: Tie in a medium sized bunch of yellow Krystal Flash, length of the body and tail. Add a short length of red Krystal Flash as a throat. Rotate the tube 180° on the vise so this becomes the belly of the fly.

Step 3: Tie in a small bunch of gold Krystal Flash along each side of body.

Step 4: Tie in a small bunch of yellow Krystal Flash on top of the tube.

Step 5: Top with a medium bunch of peacock or blue Krystal Flash.

Step 6: Complete the head with close turns of micro tinsel to match the color of topping on fly. Whip finish. Add painted eyes and cover the head with a light coat of epoxy.

Steve Shelley (Enderby, British Columbia)

Steve Shelley plays a pink salmon that hit his needlefish pattern at Coho Point, Queen Charlotte Islands. Les Johnson photo

Steve Shelley is a professional steelhead fly fishing guide on the Kispiox, Bulkley and Babine rivers of British Columbia. An experienced saltwater fly fisher as well, he is one of the first to successfully work the schools of salmon that swarm, June thru September, from the North Pacific into the shallower waters surrounding Langara, the northernmost island in the Queen Charlotte chain.

Needlefish

Tubing: 3" of 1/8" hard plastic tubing.
Thread: White Monocord.

Step 1: On top of tube, tie in a thin layer of silver Krystal Flash and cover with a thin layer of white Ocean Hair. Rotate tube on vise 180° so this part of dressing becomes belly of the Needlefish.

Step 2: Tie a thin layer of clear Krystal Flash on top of the tube.

Step 3: Lay ten strands of green Krystal Flash on top of the clear Krystal Flash.

Step 4: Cover the top of tube with a very thin layer of olive Ocean Hair, 1/4" longer than the rest of the material.

Step 5: Top with a few strands of peacock herl, a bit longer than the olive Ocean Hair.

Step 6: Finish the head by using turns of thread to create an elongated, needlefish shape. Add painted eyes and cover the head with a light coat of epoxy.

Shelley Note: "We've got every species of salmon passing through the Queen Charlottes during the summer and the Needlefish pattern has proven to be the most consistent taker for springs, coho, chum and pinkies. I guess this is why I continue to play with the dressing, trying to make it better."

Mark Waslick (Middlebury, Vermont)

Mark Waslick hoists a 25-pound roosterfish that hit his Sea Slider within 50 feet of the beach, near the northwest tip of Isla Carmen, Loreto, Mexico. Mark Mandell photo

The following patterns are Waslick's variations on the Sea Bait. Step numbers here refer to those listed in the "Basic Tying Steps" chapter.

Blue/White Sea Bait

Proceed as for the blue/green Sea Bait in **Steps 1**, **2**, and **3**. In **Step 4**, substitute silver blue FisHair for the chartreuse, and smolt blue Krystal Flash for the pearl. In **Step 5**, substitute royal blue for polar bear FisHair, and silver blue for chartreuse. In **Step 6**, dark blue Krystal Flash replaces pearl. The rest of the steps are the same.

Sea Bait Ballyhoo

This variation on the Sea Bait is tied as described in the Basic Tying Steps chapter except for the following:

Tubing: Use 2" of 1/8" hard plastic tubing and 1/2" of 3/16" vinyl tubing.

After you assemble the two sizes of tubes, slip a piece of small pearl Mylar piping over the 1/8" hard plastic tubing. Tie this down at the back end of the hard tubing with a whip finish, stretch it tight, and tie it down at the front with another whip finish. Apply Zap-A-Gap to the windings. Then proceed with **Step 1** and tie the Sea Bait. The Ballyhoo's wing is polar bear FisHair, over which is tied chartreuse Krystal Flash, then light blue FisHair, topped by aquamarine blue Krystal Flash, then silver blue FisHair, topped with light blue Krystal Flash. Sleeve the head as for the Sea Bait. Use red paint or permanent marker to color the tip of the nose. Continue with the rest of the finishing steps for the Sea Bait.

Waslick Note: "My brothers-in-law and I were fishing in the Florida Keys over a shallow reef patch for snapper and grouper and had a good chum slick going. We cast-net some ballyhoo out of the slick and my brothers-in-law began fishing them as live bait. When cero mackerel appeared all around the boat, the Ballyhoo Sea Bait outfished Deceivers, Surf Candies, deer hair and wool head flies, and *live* Ballyhoo. Sometimes as many as four or five fish were racing toward the fly at once."

Sea Bait Grizzly

This variation uses the same tube sizes, and is tied in the same steps as the basic Sea Bait pattern. The only differences are: the wing colors (polar bear FisHair, topped by silver Krystal Flash, topped by light blue FisHair, topped by aqua Krystal Flash, topped by gray FisHair, topped by black FisHair, topped by black Krystal Flash); the two grizzly saddles that are tied to the shoulders of the fly before the whip finish in **Step 1**; and the top half of the head is colored with black marker before it is sleeved with Minnow Body.

Waslick Note: "The shading with black marker under the epoxy and Mylar piping make this fly head two-tone—pearl on the underside and iridescent bright green on top."

Flexo Mirror Braid Sea Bait
Tied by Mark Mandell

Tubing: 1 1/2" of 1/8" hard plastic tubing and 1 1/4" of keyhole 1/4" O.D. vinyl tubing.
Thread: White Monocord and clear monofilament.

Step 1: Same as for basic Sea Bait.

Step 2: Tie in a piece of white yarn on the hard tubing just ahead of the join and use it to build a 3/8" long, smoothly-tapered head. Bind down the yarn with Monocord thread, trim excess, and whip finish. Cement.

Step 3: Slip a piece of 1/2" Flexo Mirror Braid over the front of the head. The braid should extend about 1 3/4" back from the tip of the nose of the fly. With monofilament thread bind down the Mirror Braid tightly at the nose of the fly. At the nose, tie in a sparse bunch of FisHair the same color and length (or close to it) as the dorsal. On top of the FisHair tie in a sparse bunch of matching Krystal Flash. Trim excess and whip finish.

Step 4: Pull the topping of FisHair and Krystal Flash down tight against the top of the Mirror Braid head, making a neat dorsal head stripe. Use a clothespin to clamp the topping to the rest of the wing at the middle of the fly—this will hold the head stripe in place while you glue it. Apply a thin coat of 5-minute epoxy over the Mirror Braid and the FisHair/Krystal Flash dorsal stripe, leaving about 1/2" of Mirror Braid and FisHair/Krystal Flash stripe uncovered at the back of the head. Let dry. Cut the excess hard tubing and material at the nose with a razor blade. Apply 1/4" yellow Witchcraft eyes. Coat the eyes with a very thin coat of epoxy. Let dry.

Mandell Note: "This shows an application of the Flexo material (See Materials chapter) to a Sea Bait pattern. The result is a fly head that has an intense silvery flash and yet allows the white undermaterial to show through its expanded mesh."

Waslick's Wool Squid

Tubing: 1 1/2" of 1/8" hard plastic tubing and 1 1/4" of 3/16" soft vinyl tubing.
Thread: White Monocord.

Step 1: Align and connect the two pieces of tubing, put them on your vise and overwrap the join area with thread. About 1/8" from the end of the soft tubing. Tie in a narrow white 4" saddle hackle with the curve pointing out. Rotate the tube and repeat with a matching feather on the opposite side.

Step 2: Over each of the saddles, tie in a 2" long, natural (off-white) marabou blood.

Step 3: Adjust the tube so the saddles and marabou are on the sides. Between the saddles, tie in a 2" long badger neck hackle. This should be tied in flat on top of the tube, with the curve pointing in.

Step 4: Rotate the tube 90° and repeat **Step 3**.

Step 5: Rotate the tube 90° and repeat **Step 3**.

Step 6: Rotate the tube 90° and repeat **Step 3**.

Step 7: Tie in about a dozen 2 1/2" strands of pearl Krystal Flash, spreading them evenly, 360° around the tube.

Step 8: On top of the tube, tie in two strands of pearl Krystal Flash, the same length as the saddles.

Step 9: Spin and pack (in the same manner as deer hair) fibers of natural colored wool fleece to make a long, tapered squid head. Whip finish.

Step 10: Trim the wool to final shape with scissors. Clip the wool close on both sides at the rear of the head (about the last 3/8") to make a flat area for the eyes.

Step 11: Epoxy 10mm doll's eyes to the head.

6

TUBE POPPERS AND SLIDERS

A dorado swims just beneath the surface, trailing a foam tube popper. Dale Edmonds photo

History

Although hook-tied fly rod poppers for bass have been manufactured for close to a century, tube poppers and sliders appear to have emerged only in the last 20 to 30 years. We say "appear to" because the available information is very sketchy. We know that Joe Butorac began making his plastic-headed Trophy Slider in 1975, and that while he came up with his ethafoam tube popper in 1965, he didn't market it commercially until 1982.

In 1987 Bob Popovics of Seaside Park, New Jersey, did away with the tube in Butorac's Pop-Eyed Popper in order to reduce the number of tying steps. Popovics' Bob's Banger popper is a simplification and modification of the Butorac pattern. The leader is slipped through a hole running the length of the popper head, rather than through a tube. And instead of being wrapped to a tube with thread, the quills of the saddle hackles are stuck

Bob Young is into a big sailfish in lumpy seas north of Isla Carmen, Sea of Cortez. The fish struck a pink and white Flexo PET popper. Les Johnson photo

into holes made in the rear of the head, epoxied, then flared out for more bulk. Popovics replaced the ethafoam head Butorac favors with a head of Live Body. He prefers the extra density of that material, and believes because of its low float in the water, it has less tendency to be pushed away by the bow wave created by the lunge of a strike. The largest diameter of Live Body he uses is 3/4". Popovics fishes his "tubeless tube" popper on bluefish and stripers, dorado, rooster-fish, and trevally. He often adds prism tape and eyes to the heads because he feels this gives the head more durability and more visibility for him, not added attraction for the fish. Popovics toothpicks his popper heads to the leader, as he doesn't want them to slide up and attract a second strike—and a line cut-off—by a following bluefish.

Most of the work covered in this chapter was done after 1991.

FOAM AND PLASTIC POPPERS/SLIDERS

Joe Butorac
Pop-Eyed Popper

Joe ties the following color variations of the popper shown in the Basic Tying Steps chapter: all-white, pink and white, green and yellow, red and white, and green and white. He uses this popper in 5/8" and 1/2" head diameters for freshwater black bass, making the body three or four inches long to simulate a shiner minnow or other large bait.

Trophy Slider

Tubing: 1/2" of 1/8" hard plastic tubing inserted into a molded, pre-painted (blue and white) plastic slider head from Trophy Tackle, 3/4" long, 1/2" in maximum diameter. A 1" long 3/16" vinyl hook holder is shoved over the hard tube and up against the back of the slider head.

Thread: Size A rod winding thread in red.

Step 1: Put the connected molded head, hard tubing, and hook holder on your vise with the side of the head facing up and attach the thread on the soft tubing just behind the join. Tie in two or three, thin 5" white saddle hackles with their curves matched and pointing inward. These feathers should be 1/3 longer than the bucktail wing.

Step 2: Rotate the tube 180° and repeat **Step 1**.

Step 3: Turn the tube so the white side of the slider head faces up. On top of the tube, tie in a medium-sized, 3 1/4" wing of white bucktail, spreading the fibers evenly around the top half of the tube.

Step 4: Rotate the tube 180°. On top of the tube, tie in a medium-sized, 3 1/4" wing of blue bucktail, spreading the fibers evenly around the top half of the tube.

Step 5: Cut a 3 1/4" piece of medium pearl Mylar piping and unravel the fibers. Rotate the tube so the side of the fly faces up. Tie in 15 or 20 Mylar fibers on top of the tube.

Step 6: Rotate the tube 180° and repeat **Step 5**.

Step 7: Trim the excess bucktail and Mylar, whip finish, and cement the wraps.

Step 8: Paint on yellow eyes with black pupils.

Butorac Note: "The heavy, molded plastic head on this slider makes it a sinking fly with a hand retrieve; when trolled behind a boat, it runs just under the surface. I tie it in all-white, pink and white, green and white, green and yellow, red and white, black and white, and yellow and white."

Mandell Note: "This fly is a bonafide trip-saver when wind or weather conditions have scattered the fish, or when the seas are too gnarly for you to stand and cast on the tiny, unrailed bow platform of a standard Baja panga."

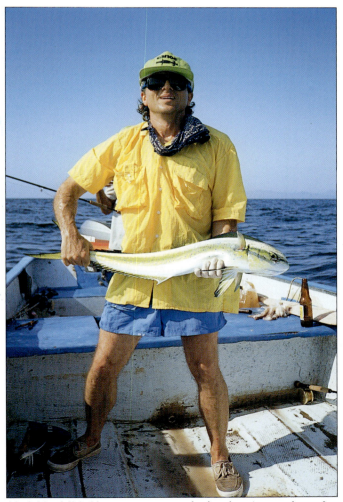

Mark Mandell holds up a popper-caught dorado prior to release. Les Johnson photo

Peter Hylander (Seattle, Washington)
Seattle Saltwater Popper

Tubing: 3/4" of 1/8" hard tubing with a 3/4" long, 3/16" vinyl hook holder.

Thread: White Monocord.

Step 1: Slide the two pieces of tubing together and put them on your vise. Attach your tying thread to the soft tubing, near its front edge, and overwrap the join area.

Step 2: Tie in three hanks of the longest, straightest white bucktail you can find. They should be at least 4" long. Each hank should be about the diameter of a pencil, and more is better in this case. Tie the first bunch onto the top of the tube, and the other two on the sides. The idea is to build a triangular base for the feathers, with no material on the bottom of the fly.

Step 3: Tie in 15 to 20 long, straight white saddle hackles, alternating from one side to the other to build up a tent-like (triangular) silhouette. Tie the feathers curving in, not out, to aid in casting these relatively bulky flies.

Step 4: If you are going to be adding any synthetics such as Krystal Flash, etc. to the dressing, this is the time to do it. Lay the material in on each side symmetrically, so the fly will not spin on the retrieve.

Step 5: Tie in an additional 15 to 20 grizzly saddle hackles in the same tented fashion as the base feathers. (Peter uses grizzly feathers dyed the same color as the popper head, and tries to use the longest ones he can find.) Do not trim off the plume at the base of the feathers, just nip off the first 1/4" or so. The plume gives the fly additional bulk.

Step 6: Whip finish the dressing, and coat it with Seam Grip or your favorite flexible adhesive.

Step 7: The larger sizes of Seattle Saltwater variegated popper heads are predrilled and countersunk at one end to take thread wraps. Push your bobbin all the way through the side of the variegated head about 3/4 back from the face—this makes a pilot hole for both doll's eyes. Dab a little glue on the thread wraps and slide on the popper head. Let the glue dry.

Step 8: Trim the doll's eyes so their posts just touch the hard tube—this makes them very durable. Apply glue to the posts and stick in the eyes.

Hylander Note: "This popper pattern reflects the synthesis of many anglers' efforts and ideas over the years."

Mark Mandell
Flexo Clear PET Popper

This is an application of Flexo material on a generic foam popper for large game fish. It uses clear Flexo PET braid and sheet pearl Mylar (available as gift wrap in greeting card stores) to create a scale and pearlescent effect on popper heads too large for the largest size of Minnow Body.

Tubing: 1 1/2" of 1/8" hard plastic tubing and 1" of keyholed 1/4" O.D. vinyl tubing.

Thread: White Monocord.

Step 1: Lining up the curves of the tubing, dab the end of the 1/8" hard plastic tubing with Zap-A-Gap and insert it into the vinyl tube 1/4". Let it dry, then put it on your vise. Overwrap the join area with thread. Tie 3" of pearl Flashabou on top of the join. Tie slightly shorter bunches of pearl Flashabou on either side of the first, spreading them to cover the sides of the tube. Cement.

Step 2: Tie in a thick, tapered bunch of 3" long white bucktail on the top of the tube. Tie slightly shorter, but equally thick, tapered bunches of white bucktail on either side of the first, spreading them to cover the sides of the tube. Trim the excess, wrap down securely and cement.

Step 3: Select three or four 3" long white saddle hackles, stack the feathers on top of each other, matching their curves, then tie them to the sides of the tube with their curved side pointing inward. Do not strip the marabou fluff from the butts of the stems before tying them in.

Step 4: Repeat **Step 3** on the other side of the fly. Tie the butts down securely with thread, trim the excess, and cement.

Step 5: On top of the tube tie in a sparse bunch of 3 3/4" long pearl Krystal Flash. On top of that, tie in a tapered bunch of 3 3/4" long polar bear FisHair. On top of that tie in another bunch of 4" long pearl Krystal Flash. On top of that goes a sparse, tapered bunch of 4" long, light blue FisHair, topped by light blue Krystal Flash. Then tie in a tapered bunch of 4" long, royal blue FisHair, topped by light blue Krystal Flash. Trim the excess, wrap with thread and cement.

Step 6: At the midline of the saddle hackles tie in six strands of pearl Krystal Flash 2" long. Do this on both sides. Trim the excess, whip finish and cement. Let dry.

Step 7: Cut a 3" by 3" square from a piece of gift wrap

sheet pearlescent Mylar. Stick a piece of metal tubing into a predrilled, blue and white painted or permanent-markered 3/4" diameter, 1 1/2" long, foam popper head. Mix up some 5-minute epoxy and spread a thin, even coat over the sides of the popper. Holding the popper by the metal tubing, place it down on the square of Mylar so the Mylar sticks out about 3/4" from one end of the popper—this will be the back of the head. Roll the Mylar onto the epoxy, or the popper onto the Mylar, smoothing it out as you go. There will be a bit of extra width on the Mylar, don't worry about it—just roll it up until the surface of the popper is covered. Let dry. Trim away the extra width of Mylar and the bit of extra at the popper face. Then make a fringe of the rear Mylar, cutting it in equal width strips to the back of the popper head.

Step 8: With a drill bit, bore out the back of the popper head to take the dressed tubing and wraps, if you have not already done so. (You can do all the boring by hand twisting a drill bit.) Measure 3/8" from the face of the popper along the midline, where the blue fades into the white, and punch a hole with your dubbing needle. Do the same on the other side of the head. Bore the holes out with a drill bit to take the posts of 10mm amber and black plastic doll's eyes. Test your doll's eyes in the holes; if their backs don't fit flush with the popper, the posts are too long—trim them with sidecutters.

Step 9: Apply 5-minute epoxy to the thread wraps on the dressed tube and insert it into the back of the popper head, making sure the head and tube are lined up correctly. Let the epoxy dry.

Step 10: Slip one end of a piece of 1/2" Flexo clear PET braid over the popper head. It should be long enough to cover the ends of the Mylar fringe. Clamp the excess Flexo an inch or so ahead of the popper face with a clothespin. Find the eye holes under the Flexo and carefully work the posts of the doll's eyes into them. Take the eyes out, mix up some more 5-minute epoxy and put a bit in and around each hole. Insert the doll's eyes back in the holes. Use a toothpick to fill any gaps between the backs of the eyes and the popper with epoxy. Let dry.

Step 11: Mix up some more epoxy and give the popper head a very thin, even coat, working it down into the braid. Don't use too much epoxy. To keep the braid from unraveling at the rear, continue spreading epoxy onto the Flexo 1/2" past the back of the popper head. Let dry. Remove the clothespin. Cut the excess Flexo from the popper face with a pair of side-cutters.

Mandell Note: "A green and yellow version (baby dorado) of this popper is shown in the color plate. It uses yellow bucktail, yellow saddles, yellow FisHair, yellow Krystal Flash, lime green FisHair, pearl Krystal Flash, dark green FisHair, and emerald green Krystal Flash. If you want to do a pink and white popper of this type, use the colors/materials/order of tube dressing for the Flexo Mirror Braid Squid, and place the eyes toward the back of the popper head."

Flexo Mirror Braid Squid

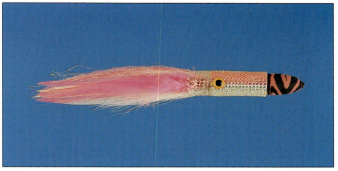

This shows an application of the Flexo Mirror Braid material to a generic, foam billfish popper.

Tubing: 2" of 1/8" hard plastic tubing and 1" of keyholed 1/4" O.D. vinyl tubing.
Thread: White 3/0.

Step 1: Dab one end of 2" of the hard tubing with Zap-A-Gap and, lining up the curves, insert it into the vinyl tubing. The overall length of the connected tubing is 2 1/2". Put the tubing on your vise. Overwrap the join area with thread, stopping about 3/4" from the back end of the tube. On top of the tube, tie in a 4 1/2" bunch of pearl Flashabou. Tie in 3 1/2" bunches of pearl Flashabou on either side of the first, spreading them evenly around the sides of tube.

Step 2: On top of the longest bunch of Flashabou, tie in a fairly thick bunch of 4 1/2" white bucktail. On either side of this, tie in slightly shorter, but equally dense bunches of white bucktail. If these last two bunches aren't enough to evenly encircle the tubing with bucktail, add a bit more bucktail. Don't cover the underside of the tube too densely, however, as that will make it difficult to stick a hook eye into the vinyl tubing—it's better to leave a slight gap there. Wrap down bucktail butts, trim the excess, and cement.

Step 3: On top of the longest bunch of bucktail, add a bunch of pink Flashabou, 6" long. On top of the Flashabou, tie in a sparse, tapered 6" length of hot pink FisHair. Trim excess and cement.

Step 4: Select four to six white 6" saddle hackles (schlappen). Don't strip off the marabou fluff at the butts. Stack the feathers on top of each other, matching their curves, then tie them in on the side of the tube, with the curved side pointing inward.

Step 5: Repeat **Step 4** for the other side of the tube. Wrap down butts, trim the excess and cement.

Step 6: Select three or four hot pink 6" saddle hackles. Leave on the marabou fluff at the butts. Stack the feathers on top of each other, matching their curves, then tie them in, curved side inward, on the side of the tube on top of the white saddles.

Step 7: Repeat **Step 6** for the other side of the tube. Wrap down butts, trim the excess and cement.

Step 8: Top the hot pink FisHair with a half dozen strands of 6" pearl Krystal Flash. On both sides of the tube, tie in ten 6" strands of lavendar Krystal Flash—they should run down the centers of the topmost hot pink saddles. Trim excess, whip finish and cement. Let dry.

Step 9: Take a 1 3/4" piece of white 3/4" diameter Live Body and drill it out to accept the tubing and then countersink one end to match the wider thread/material wraps. Mask off the underside of the head with tape and use a hot pink marker to color the dorsal area. Take a pair of plastic amber and black 10mm doll's eyes and with a pair of sidecutters trim the plastic posts to about 3/16". When the head is dry, apply 5-minute epoxy to the tube and thread wraps and insert it into the back of the head, making sure the head and tube are lined up correctly. Let the epoxy dry. Measure and mark a point 1/4" from the back of the head, along the pink/white dividing line. At this point on both sides of the head, bore out a hole for a doll's eye post with a drill bit.

Step 10: Take a long piece of 1/2" Flexo Mirror Braid. If the edge of the braid is melted together—this keeps the ends from unbraiding or expanding—trim it with scissors or sidecutters. Slip the braid over the front of the head until the ends extend past the back of the head about 3/4". Don't cut the braid, yet. Find the holes you've bored for the eye posts and, angling the clear and silver braid strands out of the way, twist the eye posts into the holes. Remove the eyes, apply 5-minute epoxy to the holes and the posts and push the eyes back in. Use a toothpick to fill gaps between backs of eyes and the braid with epoxy. Let dry.

Step 11: About one inch in front of the face of the popper pinch down the braid with a clothespin. This pulls the braid down tight around the edge of the face. Mix up more 5-minute epoxy and apply a very thin coat over the whole popper—if you use too thick a coat the silver strands won't show clearly through it. Extend the thin coat of epoxy past the back of the popper head, onto the braid about 1/2"; do this all the way around—it will keep the rear portion of the Flexo from unbraiding. Let the epoxy dry. Using sidecutters, rough trim the excess Mirror Braid from the face of the popper. Then, with scissors you don't care about (Flexo is tough stuff), do a fine trim. If there are any gaps between the edge of the face and the Mirror Braid, you can fill them with a bit more epoxy.

Mandell Note: "Les Johnson likes the stiff, flared extension behind the popper head because he thinks it increases surface disturbance on the retrieve and helps to keep the wing from fouling when the popper has to be trolled. You can also slip a small foam slider head (like the red and black Seattle Saltwater slider shown in the color plate) on the leader in front of the popper to make it track straighter when weather or sea conditions force you to troll."

Mark Waslick
Sea Popper

Tubing: 1/8" hard plastic tubing, length is equal to the slider head length plus 1/2" to 3/4", excess trimmed after the Mylar piping is attached. Hook holder is 3/8" of 3/16" vinyl tubing.
Thread: Monocord and 8/0 in white.

Step 1: Cut a piece of 5/8" diameter Live Body in two. Then ream out each of the two popper heads to take the hard and soft tubing as was done for the Sea Slider **Step 1**.

Step 2: Put together the lengths of soft and hard tubing as in **Step 1** for the Sea Bait, and wrap down the join area with thread. Apply three white saddles to each side of the tube, leaving the marabou on for a collar. Angle the saddles to form a tent or cove.

Step 3: On top of the white saddles on each side, apply three hot pink saddles with marabou in the same manner.

Step 4: Apply six to eight strands of pink Krystal Flash, the same length as the saddle hackles, to each side.

Step 5: Build a small tapered head with thread, whip finish, and Zap-A-Gap the windings.

Step 6: Paint or magic marker the dorsal surface of the head pink to match the color of the saddles. When it's dry, glue the popper head onto the tube with Zap-A-Gap. The hard tube should extend from the popper face about 1/2". In order to get a neat finish on the face of the popper, you have to concave the Live Body around the tube. You need an indent about 1/8" deep and 3/16" wide around the hard tube.

Step 7: Fray about 3 3/4" of the end of a piece of Minnow Body Large Silver/Pearl, then slip it over the popper head so the tips of the braid extend to the ends of the saddles. Stretch and tie down the Minnow Body in front of the face on the hard tube as you did for the Sea Slider. Don't worry about the folds in the Minnow Body this creates. Whip finish and Zap-a-Gap the wraps. Trim away the excess Minnow Body outside the wraps.

Step 8: With a tube slightly larger in diameter than the hard tubing (Waslick uses the barrel of a Bic pen) force the Minnow Body material and the thread wraps back into the indentation you have created in the popper face. Zap-a-Gap or epoxy 3/8" doll's eyes in place. Brush 5-minute epoxy over popper head and eyes. Trim the excess hard tubing with a razor blade.

Waslick Note: "For a blue/green popper, in **Step 2** substitute three medium blue over three bright green saddles for the hot pink, and replace the pink Krystal Flash with light blue. In **Step 6**, color the dorsal of the head blue or green. Replace the Minnow Body Large Silver/Pearl in **Step 7** with Minnow Body Large Blue/Pearl."

BALSA SLIDERS AND POPPERS

Mark Mandell

If you've ever worked with balsa wood, you know it's a light and fragile material—when coated with a waterproof finish it floats very well, but once the finish is punctured it soaks up water. Avoiding punctures is the key to keeping balsa afloat. When tied on a tube (so it slides up the line, away from teeth) and finished with a thin coat or two of epoxy, barring a leader break-off, a single balsa fly will last through dozens of large saltwater fish—if it didn't, all the work involved probably wouldn't be worth it.

Balsa requires much more preparation than plastic foam like Live Body or ethafoam (see Sea Slider and Pop-Eyed Popper): the cutting, gluing, shaping, and painting of balsa adds a good

A needlefish, up close, south of Isla Coronado, Sea of Cortez. The La Mujera tube slider shown in the photo escaped this brief encounter—a dozen others just like it in the next hour—with only minor damage to its Mylar skirt. Les Johnson photo

half hour to the hands-on time invested in each fly; to this you have to add drying time for glue and paint. On the other hand, balsa is cheap (if you don't count the necessary sealing paint, glue, your time, etc.) and it's easy to shape without a powertool. Balsa is more rigid than Live Body, so smaller and finer shapes can be achieved with it. Also, the paint used on balsa heads gives much more vivid colors than you get with permanent markers.

Since my trips to fish tropical saltwater are limited, and because anticipation is *at least* half the fun (especially when it's been wet, gray, windy, and 40 degrees for months on end here in the Pacific Northwest), I don't mind putting in the extra time to work with balsa. The goal was to produce a balsa fly that would survive countless assaults during a full day's fishing in the Sea of Cortez: one fly lasts one day.

I've never been able to find cylindrical balsa in big enough diameter to build sliders or poppers from, so I've had to make my own balsa "plywood" blocks, as described below. The blocks are probably a little bit tougher than straight balsa because of the glue layers and because you can crisscross the way the grain runs, which probably improves crush resistance.

La Mujera Slider

Tubing: 1 3/4" of 1/8" hard plastic tubing and 1" of 3/16" vinyl tubing.
Thread: Clear monofilament.

A selection of sleeved and unsleeved balsa tube poppers and sliders.

Step 1: From a sheet of 3/16" balsa, cut two 5/8" by 1 3/4" rectangles (for a small slider cut two 1/2" by 1 3/4" rectangles). These are rectangles A and D. From a sheet of 1/8" balsa, cut one 5/8" by 1 3/4" rectangle (for a small slider cut one 1/2" by 1 3/4" rectangle) and then split this rectangle in half, lengthwise. The two pieces that result are B and C.

Step 2: Spread Ambroid or some other waterproof cement on rectangles A and D, and on the sides of B and C that will touch A and D, and assemble the pieces into a block. Cut a 3" long piece of 1/8" hard tubing—this acts as a guide to help line up the pieces prior to clamping. Push the tubing between the pieces, through the center of the block. Adjust the pieces so the tube is centered in front and back, clamp them, and then remove the tube from the block. Let dry. Glue up at least a half dozen blocks at a time—it's more efficient to work with multiple heads in the gluing and painting of later steps.

Step 3: Glue different grades of sandpaper to popsicle sticks and use them to shape the balsa block. Starting with coarse paper, square off the block, then rough shape the slider. Use finer paper to get the final shape. (You could use a power tool to do the shaping. I don't use one on balsa because I like the way handshaping turns out a slightly different slider each time, and because the shape I'm fond of isn't perfectly cylindrical.) With some practice this is four minutes work. Pull a couple inches of the cotton core out of Minnow Body Large pearl (or whatever size you are using) piping and check the slider's fit inside it. You want an easy fit at this stage—the impending coats of paint will add to the slider's diameter. If you can get the slider in easily, but not out (the piping has a Chinese finger trap effect), you need to fine sand the largest diameter down a bit more. Generally speaking, a 9/16" maximum diameter head will fit Minnow Body Large pearl piping and a 3/8" diameter head (made from smaller rectangles, listed above) will fit standard Mylar extra large pearl piping. (Note: Everglow fluorescent piping is smaller in diameter than the pearlescent piping of the same size designation.)

Step 4: Cut 1 3/4" of 1/8" hard tubing and 1" of 3/16" vinyl tubing. Apply Zap-A-Gap to one end of the 1/8" tubing and insert it into 3/16" tubing about 1/4". Make sure that the natural curves of the two sizes of tubing line up with each other—other-wise the finished slider won't track straight. Ream out one end of the block with the tip of a rasp or a drill bit, so the 3/16" tubing fits into, and extends out of, what will be the rear of the head about 1/2". Check the fit of the 1/8" tubing at the end that will be the nose. If there's a large gap between the balsa and tube, mark the place where the tube exits the nose, remove the tube, then wrap it in back of the mark with thread to fit. If there's no gap, or it's small enough to fill with epoxy, smear 5-minute epoxy inside the head's cavity and on the tubing and insert the tubing into the head—again, make sure the curve is lined up. Wipe off any excess epoxy and use it to fill gaps at the nose or rear. If the balsa splits slightly at the Ambroid glue joints when you push in the tubing, work some epoxy down into the crack with the side of your dubbing needle. Let dry. If necessary, sand smooth any bumps of the dried epoxy.

Step 5: Paint the balsa head with a good, penetrating, water-proof white paint. (I push hooks into the 3/16" tubing in the back of my heads and dip them into thinned Composite Systems Floating Jig paint, then hang them on a wire in a box to drip dry thoroughly. Spray paint is fine, too.) The hobby store where you buy the balsa stock will know a brand that will work. Between coats, sand off the gloss with emery paper or steel wool, and give each head four or five thin coats of white. When the paint is dry, cover the white belly of the head with masking tape, sand the exposed dorsal lightly to get rid of the gloss, then dip, spray or brush the dorsal area (black in this case). Let it dry thoroughly, then scrape the paint clean from the hard tube at the nose and the soft tube at the rear.

Step 6: Put the painted head in your tube vise, nose first. On top of the 3/16" tubing, tie in a 2" bunch of pearl Flashabou (wet it first, so static doesn't curl it up) Then tie in 1 3/4" bunches of pearl Flashabou on either side. Spread out the Flashabou a bit so it covers all but the bottom side of the tubing. On top of the Flashabou tie in a 2 1/4" bunch of white FisHair or bucktail. On either side of this, tie in a tapered 2" bunch of white FisHair or bucktail. As with the Flashabou, spread the white FisHair or bucktail so it covers all but the bottom side of the tubing. Then, on top of the tube, add a few fibers of 2 1/4" gray FisHair or bucktail. On top of that, tie in a small bunch of pearl Krystal

Flash, same length. Then add a few fibers of 2 1/4" hot green FisHair or bucktail, topped by a small bunch of lavendar Krystal Flash, same length. On top of that, add a sparse tapered bunch of 2 1/4" olive FisHair or bucktail. Top with more lavendar Krystal Flash, the same length. Whip finish. Apply 5-minute epoxy to the wraps and to the back of the head—this seems to be where teeth punctures usually occur. Let dry.

Step 7: Put the slider in the vise, rear first. (Special Note: Make sure the paint on the head is completely dry before you try to sleeve it, otherwise the Mylar piping will stick and you'll have trouble getting it all the way down. If you can't get the piping down over your painted head on the first try, the braid will open up a bit as you work with it. Try lubricating with soap and water. If brute force fails, you have three options: 1) find some larger piping; 2) sand down the head to a smaller diameter and repaint it; or 3) forget the sleeve, stick the eyes on and epoxy it.) Pull some of the core out of Minnow Body Large pearl piping and slip it over the head until the tips of the braid extend about 1 1/2" from the back of the head. If you want to work with a shorter piece of Minnow Body, 4" of piping is plenty. Tie the Minnow Body down at the nose with a loose turn or two of mono thread. Then, holding one end of the piping, pull the other end to stretch the Mylar down into a tight cone over the nose. Wrap four or five more times with thread to lock it down securely at the nose. Whip finish. Pull the piping to the rear, drawing it down tight over the head and clamp it in place with a clothespin at the collar. Cut the excess Mylar piping and 1/8" tube, leaving about 1/4" of both protruding from the nose of the fly. Trim the Mylar piping as close as possible to the wraps. Stick on 7/32" silver Witchcraft eyes. With paint or permanent marker color red gill slits and let dry.

Step 8: Finish the head with a thin coat of 5-minute epoxy (or two coats of two-part Flexcoat epoxy rod wrap finish, or a thin coat of Aqua Seal). Depending on the type of epoxy you're using, you may have to rotate the head every few minutes to keep the finish from sagging. After it dries, trim the excess tubing in front of the thread wraps. Tease out the Mylar piping behind the head with a needle point, forming a skirt.

Mandell Note: "Mark Waslick and I fished our independently-developed, prototype Mylar-sleeved sliders, Live Body and balsa, side by side in Baja in 1992, both with good results. In the Sea of Cortez, these sliders have caught roosterfish, skipjack, dorado, cabrilla, needlefish, torito, bonito and bonita; in the Pacific Northwest saltwater they have taken coho salmon and—thanks to three years of El Niño—green mackerel. This finished fly owes much to Waslick's improved tying techniques (see his Sea Slider), which he generously shared with me.

"Though Les and I like to call this fly 'La Mujera,' it's really just a generic balsa tube slider covered with a pearlescent Mylar sleeve of Flashabou Minnow Body Large. 'La mujera' is a Spanish slang word we learned from an employee at Hotel Oasis, Loreto, Mexico who used it to describe the rather brittle temperament of a male member of our fly fishing group. We stuck the name on the slider to perpetuate the insightful remark, not to indicate an original pattern. The prismatic effect of the Mylar over the black-painted back creates an iridescent, striped green/blue (mackerel-like) color and gives the appearance of scales. We learned about this material from Lani Waller who uses it to sleeve commercially-tied wooden poppers. By altering the color of the Minnow Body piping and/or the underbody color you can get many different effects."

Fly fishers in a pair of pangas bracket a school of surface-feeding dorado, Sea of Cortez. In the lower center of the photo, a fish has just struck a tube popper cast by Bob Young. Les Johnson photo

Some of the effects you can achieve with different combinations of underpaint colors and Mylar piping. From left to right: blue dorsal/white belly sleeved with silver and pearl Minnow Body; black dorsal/white belly sleeved with pearl Minnow Body; black dorsal/white belly sleeved with copper and pearl Minnow Body; lavendar dorsal/white belly sleeved with pearl Minnow Body; hot orange dorsal/yellow belly sleeved with pearl Minnow Body; and light gray dorsal/white belly sleeved with pearl Minnow Body.

Balsa Tube Popper

This is just a minor variation on the procedure for the balsa slider.

Tubing: 1 3/4" of 1/8" hard plastic tubing and 1" of 3/16" vinyl tubing.
Thread: Clear monofilament.

Step 1: The same as for the balsa slider.
Step 2: Glue different grades of sandpaper to popsicle sticks

and use them to shape the balsa block. Starting with coarse paper, square off the block, then rough shape the popper. If you are making a cupped face popper, before you epoxy in the tubing, square off the block, and dish out the face with, in the absence of a proper tool, sandpaper wrapped around some round object of suitable size. Use finer paper to get the final shape. Pull a couple inches of the cotton core out of Minnow Body Large pearl (or whatever size you are using) piping and check the popper's fit inside it. You want an easy fit at this stage—the impending coats of paint will add to the popper's diameter.

Step 3: Cut 1 3/4" of 1/8" hard tubing and 1" of 3/16" soft tubing. Apply Zap-A-Gap to one end of the 1/8" tubing and insert it into 3/16" tubing about 1/4". Make sure that the natural curves of the two sizes of tubing line up with each other—otherwise the finished popper won't track straight. Ream out one end of the block with the tip of a rasp or a drill bit, so the 3/16" tubing fits into, and extends out of, what will be the rear of the head about 1/2". Check the fit of the 1/8" tubing at the end that will be the face. If there's a large gap, mark the place where the tube exits the face, remove the tube, then wrap it in back of the mark with thread to fit. If there's no gap, or it's small enough to fill with epoxy, go ahead and smear 5-minute epoxy inside the head's cavity and on the tubing and insert the tubing into the head—again, make sure the curve is lined up. Wipe off any excess epoxy and use it to fill gaps at face or rear. If the balsa splits slightly at the Ambroid glue joints when you push in the tubing, work some epoxy down into the crack with the side of your dubbing needle. Let dry. If necessary, sand smooth any bumps of the dried epoxy. Use a razor blade to cut off the excess 1/8" tubing flush with the face.

Step 4: As with the balsa slider, give the head four or five coats of a good white waterproof sealer, letting it dry thoroughly and sanding lightly between each coat. Then paint the popper whatever final color or colors you want. Let dry.

Step 5: Put the painted head on your vise, face first. On top of the 3/16" tubing, tie in 2" of pearl Flashabou (wet it first, so static doesn't curl it up). Then tie in 1 3/4" of pearl Flashabou on either side. Spread out the Flashabou a bit so it covers all but the bottom side of the tubing. On top of the Flashabou tie in 2 1/4" of white bucktail. On either side of this, tie in 2" white bucktail. As with the Flashabou, spread the white bucktail so it covers all but the bottom side of the tubing. Then, on either side of the tube, add four white saddle hackles 2 1/4" long—or two matched white marabou bloods, one to a side, 2 1/4" long. Whip finish. Apply 5-minute epoxy to the wraps, letting it flow up onto the back of the head as with slider. Let dry.

Step 6: Put the popper on the vise, rear first. The procedure for sleeving a popper with Mylar piping is the same as for the slider, except with a popper you whip finish with mono thread only at the collar, and leave about a 1/4" of excess piping overhanging the face. Tips of the Mylar braid should extend about 1 1/2" from the rear of the head. Try to size your popper so that after painting you get a nice tight fit at the edge of the face. If

your popper is too small for the sleeve, or if it doesn't fit tightly at the face or elsewhere, and you can't adjust the fit by pulling and clamping it with a clothespin, you can wrap it down with a few turns of mono thread as you pull the piping tight. If you've had to use use mono to adjust the fit, stick on the 7/32" silver Witchcraft eyes and overwrap them with thread as for the slider, then whip finish; if not, just stick the eyes on. Paint or permanent marker the red gill slits.

Step 7: One coat of epoxy may not be enough to hide the adjustment wraps of mono, if you're fussy about such things. If you're using a two-part rod wrap epoxy like FlexCoat, it will flow through the Mylar braid and fill the gap at the face nicely. Depending on the type of epoxy you are using, you may have to rotate the head every few minutes to keep the finish from sagging. And whatever kind of epoxy you are using for the head, don't put it on the popper face, yet. After the epoxy on the piping has set up, use scissors to trim away excess Mylar piping from the edge of the popper face. Then apply a coat of epoxy to the popper face as well. After it dries, tease out the Mylar piping behind the head with a needle point, forming a skirt.

Mandell Note: "If you're making a paint-only (unsleeved) popper or slider, after **Step 4** above, cut a short piece of Minnow Body Large pearl piping (or in the case of smaller pencil poppers, extra large regular pearl Mylar piping) and slip it up over the hair, feather, and Flashabou collar. Adjust the piping to the desired length at the rear, then tie it down over the 5-minute epoxied collar with mono thread. Trim the excess Mylar as close as possible to the back of the popper or slider head, then make a neat overwrap and whip finish. Apply the stick-on Witchcraft eyes. The coat (or coats, if you're using FlexCoat) of finish epoxy is put on over the mono thread as well as the painted balsa head. After the coat of epoxy has set, fray out the back end of the piping to make a Mylar skirt. A paint-only balsa head, even with two coats of FlexCoat epoxy finish, isn't as durable as a painted, Mylar sleeved, and epoxied head."

T U B E   F L I E S

Dear Fellow Tube Fly Tier,

We want to know what you're tying. If you come up with a winner of a tube fly, send us a copy of the pattern, tell us what it's working on, and include tying instructions, and, if possible, a color 35mm slide of yourself and a tube-caught fish. The address is:

Tube Flies
℅ Les Johnson
1924 E. Fir Street
Seattle, Washington 98122 (USA)

APPENDIX OF SOURCES

W. T. Humphries and Sons, Ltd., Poughill, Bude, Cornwall, England
Manufacturer of "Slipstream" metal and plastic tubes designed for fly tying.

Joe Butorac, Trophy Tackle, Inc., P.O. Box 98, Arlington, WA 98223
Professional tube fly tier, sells kits with popper heads, eyes, and tubing.

Traun River Products, Hauptstrasse 4-6, 83313 Siegsdorf, West Germany
Manufacturer of wing and body materials, aluminum tubes, tying supplies.

Techflex, Inc., P.O. Box 119, 50 Station Road, Sparta, NJ 07871
Manufacturer of Flexo and Flexo Mirror Braid.

Dale Clemens Custom Tackle, 444 Schantz Rd., Allentown, PA 18104
Manufacturer of Live Body foam for popper and slider heads.

Peter Hylander, Seattle Saltwater, P.O. Box 19416, Seattle, WA 98109
Manufacturer of tube fly vise adaptors and variegated foam tube popper heads and popper kits.

Partridge of Redditch, Redditch, B97 4JE England
Manufacturer of hooks for tube flies, SLF seal substitute.

Kennebec River Fly and Tackle Co., P.O. Box 452, South Freeport, ME 04078
Manufacturer of the Bill Hunter tube fly tying tool.

Jack Moore, Fishunter, Inc., 19808 144th Place South East, Renton, WA 98058
Wholesaler of fly tying tools and materials.

Jack Perry, Perry Design, 7401 Zircon Drive S.W., Tacoma, WA 98498
Manufacturer of the Jack Perry tube fly vise.

Umpqua Feather Merchants, P.O. Box 700, Glide, OR 97443
Manufacturers of flies and distributor of Tiemco hooks and fly tying materials.

Davy Wotton, Heron House, Station Road, Griffithstown, Pontypool, Gwent, Wales, Great Britain NP4 5ES
Professional fly tier, fly tying teacher, lecturer.

Rod Yerger, P.O. Box 294, Lawrence, PA 15055
Professional fly tier, sells tube components and tying materials.

INDEX

More Helpful Books for Fishing and Fly Tying

FEDERATION OF FLY FISHERS FLY PATTERN ENCYCLOPEDIA
Over 1600 of the Best Fly Patterns
Edited by Al & Gretchen Beatty

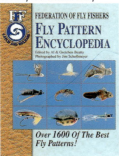

Simply stated, this book is a Federation of Fly Fishers' conclave taken to the next level, a level that allows the reader to enjoy the learning and sharing in the comfort of their own home. The flies, ideas, and techniques shared herein are from the "best of the best" demonstration fly tiers North America has to offer. The tiers are the famous as well as the unknown with one simple characteristic in common; they freely share their knowledge. Many of the unpublished patterns in this book contain materials, tips, tricks, or gems of information never before seen.

As you leaf through these pages, you will get from them just what you would if you spent time in the fly tying area at any FFF function. At such a show, if you dedicate time to observing the individual tiers, you can learn the information, tips, or tricks they are demonstrating. All of this knowledge can be found in *Federation of Fly Fishers Fly Pattern Encyclopedia* so get comfortable and get ready to improve upon your fly tying technique with the help of some of North America's best fly tiers. Full color, 8 1/2 x 11 inches, 232 pages.

SB: $39.95   ISBN: 1-57188-208-1

FLY FISHING AFOOT IN THE SURF ZONE
Ken Hanley

You'll find facts and advice on: Chum salmon, rockfish, cabezon, striped bass, surfperch, Pacific bonito, corbina, croaker, flatfish, sand bass, lingcod, and silver salmon; over 80 locations in Washington, Oregon, California, and Northern Baja; 21 fly patterns and full recipes, with angling tips for each fly; plus tips on equipment, water-reading skills, tides and moon phases, and field references for the traveler.

Ken Hanley is a pioneering spirit, with enthusiasm and excitement he shares his vast knowledge of Pacific Coast fly angling as only he can. You will get the insight you need to be a success at this "wild" game. 8 1/2 x 11 inches; 47 pages.

SB: $8.95   ISBN: 1-57188-177-8

TYING SALTWATER FLIES: 12 OF THE BEST
Deke Meyer

Fishing in saltwater is a challenge for many reasons, but now thanks to this book, one aspect—the most productive flies to use—is no longer a problem. Meyer presents 12 different saltwater fly designs—all of them "hot," all of them simple enough for a beginner to tie. Included are flies representing the food of saltwater fish, from crustacean to prey fish. All-color, 8 1/2 x 11 inches, 32 pages.

SB: $9.95   ISBN: 1-57188-066-6

SIGHT-FISHING FOR STRIPED BASS
Alan Caolo

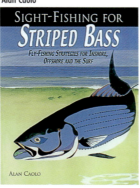

Long thought to be exclusively a tropical experience, anglers have begun exploring flats-fishing opportunities for striped bass. In this book, Caolo has created the definitive text on this growing sport. Spectacular photography and clear text illustrate such topics as: sight-fishing waters; striped bass behavior; fly patterns; naturals; spotting the fish; presentations and retrieves; angling strategies; tackle equipment; destinations; and more. Sandy Moret says Caolo understands his subject "light years beyond anything I've ever read on the subject . . ." Jeffrey Cardenas calls it "the definitive account," and Nick Curcione says, ". . . must reading . . . well-written, thoroughly researched, and replete with detailed information . . . " 8 1/2 x 11 inches, 100 pages, full-color.

SB: 25.00   ISBN: 1-57188-253-7
HB: $39.95   ISBN: 1-57188-257-X

SALTWATER GAME FISHES OF THE WORLD
Bob Dunn and Peter Goadby

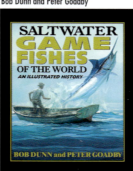

This is a book for all those who love the sea and the great oceanic and inshore fishes which inhabit it. It is a book, not only for anglers, but for marine scientists, nature lovers and seafarers of all nations who share a curiosity about these majestic creatures and how our knowledge of them slowly developed over the past two millennia. A 2000 year history of the early naturalist and fishes they first described. Illustrations are intensely evocative of the period and remind us of the skills of yesteryear, now largely lost. There is the never-told-before history of the ancient sport of sea fishing from its origins in the mists of antiquity to the present day. All color, 9.5 x 12.5 inches, 304 pages.

HB: $25.00   ISBN: 1-86513-010-9

SMELT FLY PATTERNS
Donald A. Wilson

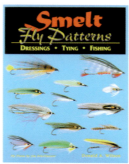

Many different fish feed on smelt, so consequently they are very important to fly fishermen. And because they can be found in many waters around the world, *everyone* has a favorite smelt pattern! Never before has an entire book been dedicated to this species, and the most productive flies and techniques to use when fishing their imitations, *Smelt Fly Patterns* is all you need to fish these flies with great success! Color fly plates 8 1/2 x 11 inches, 64 pages.

SB: $19.95   ISBN: 1-57188-071-2

THE FLY TIER'S BENCHSIDE REFERENCE TO TECHNIQUES AND DRESSING STYLES
Ted Leeson and Jim Schollmeyer

Printed in full color on top-quality paper, this book features over 3,000 color photographs and over 400,000 words describing and showing, step-by-step, hundreds of fly-tying techniques! Leeson and Schollmeyer have collaborated to produce this masterful volume which will be the standard fly-tying reference book for the entire trout-fishing world. Through enormous effort on their part they bring to all who love flies and fly fishing a wonderful compendium of fly-tying knowledge. Every fly tier should have this book in their library! All color, 8 1/2 by 11 inches, 464 pages, over 3,000 color photographs, index, hardbound with dust jacket.

HB: $100.00   ISBN: 1-57188-126-3

SALTWATER FLIES: OVER 700 OF THE BEST
Deke Meyer

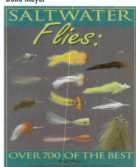

An all-color fly dictionary of the very best saltwater flies for inshore and ocean use. Effective flies for all saltwater game fish species. Photographed large, crisp and in true color by Jim Schollmeyer. Pattern recipes next to each fly. This is a magnificent book featuring the largest display of working saltwater fly patterns! 8 1/2 x 11 inches, 119 pages.

SB: $24.95   ISBN: 1-57188-020-8

CURTIS CREEK MANIFESTO
Sheridan Anderson

Finest beginner fly-fishing guide due to its simple, straightforward approach. It is laced with outstanding humor provided in its hundreds of illustrations. All the practical information you need to know is presented in an extremely delightful way such as rod, reel, fly line and fly selection, casting, reading water, insect knowledge to determine which fly pattern to use, striking and playing fish, leaders and knot tying, fly tying, rod repairs, and many helpful tips. A great, easy-to-understand book. 8 1/2 x 11 inches, 48 pages.

SB: $7.95   ISBN: 0-936608-06-4

Ask for these books at your local fly/tackle shop or call toll-free to order:
1-800-541-9498 (8-5 p.s.t.) • www.amatobooks.com
Frank Amato Publications, Inc. • P.O. Box 82112 • Portland, Oregon 97282

0061